A MEDAL FOR LIFE

A MEDAL FOR LIFE

Biography of
Capt Wm. Leefe Robinson, VC

Leslie Wm. Bills

SPELLMOUNT LIMITED
TUNBRIDGE WELLS
KENT

First published in the UK in 1990 by
Spellmount Ltd, Publishers
12 Dene Way, Speldhurst
Tunbridge Wells, Kent TN3 0NX
ISBN 0-946771-56-1

British Library Cataloguing in Publication Data
Bills, Leslie William, *1926-*
A medal for life: biography of Captain William Leefe
    Robinson.
    1.   World war 2. Air operations by Great Britain. Royal
    Air Force – biographies
    I.   Title   II. Series
    940.54'4941'0924

Typesetting by Vitaset, Paddock Wood, Kent
Printed in Great Britain by PPC Limited
Leatherhead, Surrey

ACKNOWLEDGMENTS

My grateful thanks for the help and assistance given to me, and letters of memories rekindled after so many years: Miss Rose Coombs, MBE, Researcher, English Heroes, (Special Collection Office, Imperial War Museum, London). Mrs Pat Mamprin, (Isle of Wight), Old Cottonian Association. *Daily Express*, Fleet Street, London EC4 for publishing my original letter of my mother's friendship with Leefe Robinson. P M K Michell, Manager of Jumboor Estate, (1947-57), Co-org, India, for his valuable information on India and the coffee plantations of Co-org. John Hart, Librarian, Redbridge Library, Ilford. John Barfoot (Society of World War I Aero Historians). Mrs Majorie Main-Waddell for her great interest, photographs and encouragement. Mrs F Watts. Mrs E L Wilson for her early recollections of Leefe Robinson's schooldays. Mrs Ivy W Varny. Mrs C B Shepherd. George Critchlow. Muriel F Leefe. Lilian Scott. Thora Edwards (Canada), for her recollections of events. Lionel (John) F Dee (ex-pilot 1941). Olive Sherwin. Roy E Knowles. Phyllis Aplin. Harold Robinson (New Zealand). G Godfrey. Lily Thomas. Welwyn Hatfield District Council for the copy of the commemorative brochure for the ceremony of unveiling of the restored *Daily Express* Leefe Robinson/Airship Memorial at Cuffley in 1986. My thanks to Mrs Rose David (daughter of Irene Ross, née Leefe Robinson), for the many photographs and documentation from the family archives, which have proved invaluable to the production of this book.

I would also like to acknowledge the valuable information provided by Messrs Christie's of St James's, London, and for their permission to use extracts from their catalogues and brochures.

I am also grateful to the Trustees of The Imperial War Museum for permission to reproduce photographs.

I am indebted to all the many people who sent letters, for the great interest shown and for sharing their memories with my mother and myself for the long-forgotten happenings of 'Zepp Sunday'; for the support of my wife, Pat, in deciphering my scribbled notes; and to Pat Adams for editing and typing the final manuscript. Line drawings: thanks to Janes Information Group. Photographs of Ilford before and after: thanks to London Borough of Redbridge, Local History Library, for permission to produce.

My final acknowledgment and thanks to Mrs Gia Libin for her agreement to entitle this book of the biography of her uncle, Capt William Leefe Robinson, VC *A Medal for Life*, being the name of the charity for the financial help to children suffering with Leukemia.

In the Spellmount Military list:

The Territorial Battalions – A pictorial history
The Yeomanry Regiments – A pictorial history
Over the Rhine – The Last Days of War in Europe
History of the Cambridge University OTC
Yeoman Service
The Fighting Troops of the Austro-Hungarian Army
Intelligence Officer in the Peninsula
The Scottish Regiments – A pictorial history
The Royal Marines – A pictorial history
The Royal Tank Regiment – A pictorial history
The Irish Regiments – A pictorial history
British Sieges of the Peninsular War
Victoria's Victories
Heaven and Hell – German paratroop war diary
Rorke's Drift
Came the Dawn – Fifty years an Army Officer
Kitchener's Army – A pictorial history
On the Word of Command – a pictorial history of the Regimental Sergeant Major
Marlborough – As Military Commander

In the Military Machine list:

Napoleon's Military Machine
Falklands Military Machine
Wellington's Military Machine

In the Nautical list:

Sea of Memories
Evolution of Engineering in the Royal Navy Vol I 1827-1939
In Perilous Seas

In the Aviation list:

Diary of a Bomb Aimer
Operation 'Bograt' – From France to Burma

CONTENTS

APPENDICES

Christie's Medal Department
request the pleasure of your company
on Monday 21st November 1988
at a private view
in their Great Rooms
of the William Leefe Robinson Exhibition
including the Victoria Cross Group
to be sold in London on Tuesday 22nd November 1988

R.S.V.P.
Miss Sarah Richardson
Christie's
8 King Street, St. James's   *6.00 p.m. – 8.00 p.m.*
London SW1   *Please bring this invitation with you*

BIBLIOGRAPHY

Richthofen and His Flying Circus by H J Nowarra & Major Kimbrough Brown (Harleyford, 1958)

The Red Air Fighter by Manfred Freiherr von Richthofen (The Aeroplane & General Publishing Co, 1918)

Sagittarius Rising by Cecil Lewis 1914-18 (Penguin, 1977)

The Tunnellers of Holzminden by H G Durnford, 1920 (Cambridge University Press, 1930)

Hornchurch During the Great War by Chas. Thomas Perfect (Benham and Co Ltd, Colchester, 1920)

Air Fighting 1914-18 by Peter Simkins. (Imperial War Museum, 1978)

Exhibition Catalogue of Victoria Cross Group awarded to Captain William Leefe Robinson, Royal Flying Corps, 1988. Christie Manson & Woods Ltd)

World War I by Sir John Hammerton

DEDICATION

*To my daughters and in memory
of my mother.*

Letter from Mrs R G Libin, Chairman of Charitable Trust,
A MEDAL FOR LIFE

(L)

Fairways.
1 Fox Hill Close
Haywards Heath
W. Sx RH16 4RA.
Oct 19ᵗʰ 1988.

Dear Leslie Bells,
        I was enchanted with
your letter and newspaper
cutting and needless to say I
would be delighted if you would
be kind enough to write my
Uncle's story. By all means call
it "A Medal for Life" because
after all these brave young men
died so that we could all live. .
        I am enclosing information
that may be of interest to you.
                Yours Sincerely
                    Gia Libin

1 Co-org, Southern India

It is difficult to imagine a more idyllic place in which to bring up a young boy than the tiny state of Co-org in Southern India. An area of just 60 kilometres square, perched on the western ghats, with a salubrious climate, and enjoying a unique position shaded by mountains and forests. Three and a half thousand feet above sea level, Co-org is a coffee growing state because, unlike tea which requires to be grown in the open, the plants needed shade and the area was ideal for the flourishing plantations.

In an area where man and nature had combined their efforts with such harmony, William Leefe Robinson was born on 14 July 1895, the youngest of seven children of Horace Robinson, owner of the Kaima Betta estate. A decade before the turn of the century the European planters built, for their spiritual guidance, Christchurch in Pollibetta, and proceeded to transform the wild district into the lush green of many coffee plantations. William's father was probably one of the last private coffee planters in the district. Many plantation owners who had met financial problems mortgaged their estates by borrowing from the East India Company – Mathesons – and when they could not meet their commitments the Company would foreclose, and they obtained many estates in this way. Later they were to become the Coffee Planters Association. Horace Robinson, with considerable expertise in the management of a plantation, retained his independence, his assiduous strivings ensuring the coffee industry in that part of the world would permanently raise the status of India as a leading supplier.

William, as a baby boy, was adored by his four older sisters and his idyllic childhood years gave him a sense of fun, with brother Harold and indulgent parents accepting his pranks with loving benevolence. It is recollected that he was always up to jokes and at lessons the family governess was asked the most awkward questions, especially in scripture!

In 1901 a trip to England found his good nature curtailed with the long journey by sea, and the formalities of schooling at the Dragon School in Oxford, but soon he returned to India and his parents to commence studies at Bishops Cotton School in Bangalore. William's sister taught in the same school and was a great friend of Mrs K L Robertson (née Scott), the headmistress of the Kindergarten.

Horace Robinson, William's father, *c*1878   *Mrs R. David*

Lt Francis Robinson RN, 1846-94, with M. Georgina Partridge.
Horace Robinson's eldest brother, *c*1881   *Mrs R. David*

Dr Mark Robinson, brother of William's father, 1849-1914. Married
Elizabeth Limnell, *c*1888   *Mrs R. David*

William Brabham Robinson, 1882. Chief Constructor RN. William's grandfather. Photo taken the year his father married Elizabeth Leefe   *Mrs R. David*

William's mother, Elizabeth Leefe, *c*1880

Tennis 'at home' at 'Kaima Betta', S. Co-org, India. Home of the Leefe Robinson family, Nov 1901 *Mrs R. David*

The family ties were very strong and, although his early education was sparse and unco-ordinated, his sense of fun saw him over most difficulties. It was not an uncommon sight to see the girls on their upright bicycles, riding through the plantation paths which ran to and fro down steep slopes of a maze of colour, with mischievous 'Billy' racing after them; the distant wild heliotrope-covered scrubland like a purple carpet before them, past white-walled buildings, brightened with masses of red poinsettias and cascades of bougainvillea.

Occasionally, young William would cycle with his father and older brother, Harold, to Topal, some 10 kilometres distant through the most beautiful countryside: long paddy valleys and green, forested glades with tall, silver oak trees fringing the coffee plantations. The return journey was a relaxing, downhill indulgence, soaking up the beauty of the district. It is difficult to imagine that this perfect canvas of his young life was just the beginning of a great adventure which would bring him fame, fortune, the horror of war, and an untimely death!

Father was not only a successful planter, but the Editor of *The Bangalore Daily Post*, which was situated opposite the Imperial Bank in Museum Road, Bangalore. The planters would frequent the Bamboo Club for their 'Sundowners' to discuss matters of the day, and to 'put the world to rights' – not the least subject of which was the Lloyd George Budget of 1909 and his potential legislation for the imposition of super tax on the incomes of the very rich.

2 Boyhood to manhood

In August 1909, William returned to England with his brother Harold for more serious studies at St Bees College, Cumbria. St Bees School was founded in 1586 by Charter granted by Queen Elizabeth I in 1583 to the Archbishop of Canterbury for the benefit of boys residing in Cumberland and Westmorland. In the mid-19th century, the school attracted many boarding pupils from far afield, and Billy and Harold took up residence in Eaglesfield House.

William struggled with his academic studies and found the lessons hard, being overshadowed by Harold, who attained a third place from the top of the form, and this bothered William. His academic failures were many, and successes were few, but he was a fit lad and, with great spirit, overcame his disappointments with a gradual advancement on the sports field.

He soon met the Braidford brothers, of whom three of the six brothers, Frank, Bill and Percy, became close friends. Later Bill and Percy were to be killed on the Somme in France, shortly after Percy had been awarded the Military Cross for outstanding bravery.

Billy and Harold spent some of their holidays in Keswick, travelling by train to the home of Mrs Wise. Set in the delightful countryside of Cumbria, the boys relaxed from the rigours of boarding school life, mischievously casting a youthful eye over the local beauties. Here they met the attractive and personable Ruby Jenkinson. Her friends, Doris Iredale and Ethel Waters encouraged the flirtatious affairs with the boys. They needed little prompting, having an intuitive understanding of the opposite gender.

As a teetotaller and non-smoker, Billy's interests were both extensive and talented. He played various musical instruments and had a good singing voice. Distracted easily by a pretty face, he had little interest in the mundane tasks of the school curriculum.

Outside the classroom, William excelled at sports; won a house cap for football and, at all events in the open air, showed excellence; his hockey and sculling skills overshadowing any fears of inability to settle to an academic career.

Kitty Robinson (Gia Libin's mother) third from left, and Irene (Rose David's mother) far right, with friends in Russia, *c*1912
Mrs R. David

William's sister Irene and Baroness Von Der Recke in Kurland,
Russia, Jan 1913   *Mrs R. David*

William and Irene at St Bees School, Cumberland, April 1913
Mrs R. David

William's sister, Grace 'G' and her husband Arthur Limnell
Robinson, 2/Lt, Northamptonshire Battalion who died of wounds on
the Western front, Battle of Mons, 20 Feb 1916   *Mrs R. David*

Regular contact with his parents in Pollibetta expressed his longing to return to the district of his birth, obviously missing the happy times of his young life, as he tried to come to terms with the traumas and hardships of a boarding school. He remembered the beauty and tranquility of Co-org, with the ethereal quality of the native women, its tall handsome men, the singing in the plantations as they busied themselves with the crop, and the climate. Why did it always rain in Cumberland just as you took to the field? He loved every detail of his birthplace and missed his mother in particular. He wrote to her on one occasion: 'I often wonder if I will make a mess of my life – in a way of failing exams', concerned that other scholars had received a more sound, earlier education than he had been privileged to enjoy. His fears were forgotten briefly during a holiday in Russia with the Baroness von der Recke, which was so enjoyable to 'young Billy', he failed to return to St Bees College until three weeks of the autumn term of 1912 had slipped quietly into history.

William's last year at St Bees was his best as, no longer feeling he was in competition with his brother, Harold, he progressed to become Head Boy of Eaglesfield House. His first real taste of leadership!

His success on the sports field, his good looks, but shy nature, made him a very noticeable young man on the rare occasions when he was in the company of young ladies. In the uniform of the Officers' Training Corps he became even more attractive, swiftly rising to the rank of sergeant and feeling for the first time the stirrings of a young man with a pride in his appearance and thoughts for the future.

Harold Robinson, 'Kaima Betta' Estate, c1920

The Robinson Girls, 'Kaima Betta', Co-org, Southern India. From left to right: Grace, friend, Ruth, Horace Robinson (father), Irene, Kitty, friend, *c*1920   *Mrs R. David*

Bishops Cotton School, Bangalore, 1989   *Trixie Pachy*

He had his first experience of army life at a camp at Mytchett, Surrey (near Aldershot). Most of his holidays were spent in Bournemouth with his sister, Kitty, but he longed to travel again and, in January 1913, he wrote to his mother expressing a desire to go to France with his sister to increase his knowledge of the French language, being very conscious of the slow progress of his education as well as the competition of his compatriots, all of whom were quite oblivious to the foreboding, international rumblings and political intrigue looming ahead.

In April 1914, at the age of 18 years, he longed to leave school, and with private tutorship gained entry into Sandhurst Military Academy, hoping to obtain a commission in the Indian Army. He assured his mother that if the climate in India was not to his liking he would try the English Army or, with luck, the Egyptian Army, with the help of influential friends. His letters to home expressed his own untried ambitions, his apprehension of the untrod course of his life, but showed confidence and enthusiasm for the future.

The Robinson family went about its business in the early part of 1914 with the hopes and aspirations of many a large family of girls and boys. Will the girls marry? Which careers for the boys? Is the crop going to be a success this year?

Two of the girls did marry: Grace to Arthur Linell Robinson, her cousin, who was later to work in West Africa as a mining engineer: and Ruth married John Irwin, a bachelor of mature years, who managed the Jumboor Coffee Estate in the northern province of Co-org. At that time a young man, Michael Michell, was learning the trade on the estate, which was owned by a Douglas Tweedie, (Ruth and John were to retire in 1920 and return to England to live in Brighton.)

Harold returned to India, after being successful at his academic studies, to follow in his father's footsteps to manage a Tea Estate.

Kitty longed to return to Russia as governess to Baroness von der Recke.

2/Lt William Leefe Robinson commissioned from the Royal Military
College, Sandhurst into the Worcester Regt in 1914 and posted to
Fort Tregantle, Cornwall

3 Serajevo

On Sunday, 28 June 1914, Archduke Franz Ferdinand, the Austro-Hungarian Heir Presumptive, and his morganatic wife, the Duchess of Hohenburg, with their entourage, were on their way to a reception at the Town Hall in Serajevo, the capital of Bosnia. Their route took them over three bridges spanning the River Milyatsa. Conspirators were at each bridge, and near the first one a bomb was thrown at the Archduke's car by an individual described as a compositor from Trevinje (a garrison town in the extreme south of Herzegovina). The Archduke warded off the missile with his arm and it exploded behind the car, injuring one of the attendants in the second car. The rest of the party drove on to the Town Hall where the Mayor, ignorant of the untoward happening, made a speech of welcome, only to be interrupted by the Archduke with a sarcastic reference to a welcome with bombs!

The Archducal pair then drove to the hospital to visit the wounded attendant. As a measure of safety the route was changed but, unfortunately for the world, by mistake (or design) the driver of the leading car kept to the original route, turning into Franz Josef Street instead of going straight on. The Governor of Bosnia called out to the driver of the Archduke's car that he was going in the wrong direction and he braked hard, causing a momentary stoppage of the entourage. At that moment a young Bosnian student named Gavrilo Princip dashed forward and shot twice at the Archduke with his Browning pistol. The first bullet hit the Archduke and the second the Duchess, who had flung herself forward to protect her husband. She was dead by the time they reached the hospital, and the Archduke died ten minutes later, just after 11.00am. The day was the anniversary of the wedding of this unfortunate couple.

The complexity of the Serajevo affair threatened the Austria-Hungary triple alliance with Italy and Germany, and the Russian and Serbian Pan Slavian agitation brought the world closer to bloodshed. The 25 prisoners concerned with the crime soon found themselves being defended in a political arena with, seemingly, the blame put firmly on the Serbians for their attempt to liberate Bosnia and Herzegovina from Austrian domination. Only one month elapsed between the murder at Serajevo and the first declarations of war between Austria, Serbia and Russia, and then

Germany, Russia and France, and those 30 days were filled with diplomatic and other exchanges.

On 2 August 1914 Germany made a formal demand for permission to march her troops through Belgium. This was emphatically refused and Albert, King of the Belgians, made a direct appeal to King George V, who sent a request to Berlin on 4 August for assurance that the demand made upon Belgium should not be proceeded with and that her neutrality be respected. A reply was asked for by 11.00pm that night (midnight by German time). As the German Government gave no reply, Great Britain and Germany were at war when the hour struck.

Historians have recorded all the complex details of the events which led up to the declaration of war between Great Britain and Germany, but it could be said that a 'mistake' by an unknown chauffeur in a far-off country sealed the fate of William Leefe Robinson, condemning this young man – handsome, charming, heroic, and with a great zest for life – to an iniquitous and very untimely death, along with the many others who lost their lives through the First World War. He symbolizes all the utter futility of war!

Ten days after the declaration of war on 4 August 1914 William Leefe Robinson entered Sandhurst, aged 19 years. He was gazetted on 16 December to the Worcester Regiment, where he joined the Fifth Militia Battalion and was posted to Tregantle, Cornwall, commissioned as a Second Lieutenant.

BE 2c Aeroplane (maximum speed 72mph)   *Imperial War Museum*

4 Call to Arms

The German army stormed through Belgium with all the might of a great, victorious invader, crushing the majority of the country by the end of August 1914. The Germans advanced in hordes, attacking in rushes, and suffered appalling casualties, fighting in close formation and losing men from the defenders' machine guns and artillery fire. In the air, however, the enemy had the highest hopes for the use of the destructive power of their Zeppelins, and the huge, cigar-shaped monsters wrought havoc in Belgium.

As a young officer, William found life both boring and tedious, although he found that special reserve men were less difficult to manage than the raw recruits brought in by Lord Kitchener's 'Call to Arms'. As Orderly Officer of a Company commanded by a drunken Captain, his aspirations of a military career began to diminish, with the tedium of ensuring the discipline of men who were bored with inactivity.

With the removal of his superior and the additional responsibility of his command, 2/Lt Leefe Robinson brightened at his possible transfer to West Africa, with its increased remuneration of £25 a month, plus other benefits and allowances. Restlessly, he wanted to get to a fighting unit to help his friends who were defending the country, but his youthful years precluded the authorities from sending him to a zone where he could 'avenge the deaths' of many of his colleagues from school, in particular 'Nailer' Hawkesworth, who had been a great friend.

On 19/20 January 1915 two airships bombed East Anglia, the first of many to attack this country and its people, although in the previous October a squadron of British aeroplanes had dropped bombs on The Zeppelins' home base – one bomb dropped from 500ft, causing a direct hit on an enormous hangar at Dusseldorf.

The tales of trench warfare permeated through to the men. The Battle of Aisne in September 1914; the early start of static, trench strategy, where trenches were to remain for three or four years of ceaseless fighting in conditions of privation difficult to imagine. Field guns pounding the enemy in a carpet of destruction – neither tree nor building surviving; of turbaned Indian troops fighting side by side with British soldiers in a duck-board swamp, where they fought and died in climatic conditions so different, and far, from their homeland.

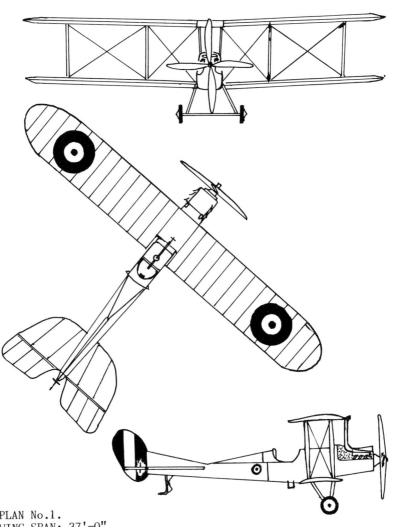

PLAN No.1.
WING SPAN: 37'-0".
LENGTH: 27'-3".

R.A.F. B.E. 2a

But the period of waiting dragged on through the winter of 1915, doing guard duties, superintending the digging of trenches, and keeping a restless battalion interested in the routine tasks of the day. He frequently wrote to his mother, longing to see Co-org, and dwelling constantly on thoughts of his marriage, albeit he found it difficult to imagine a girl who would be as sweet as his 'dear old mater'.

William's desire for action and his patriotic upbringing to defend his country forced him to try every avenue to get to the fighting zones, and he could see merit in an attempt to transfer to the Royal Flying Corps. His application was answered quickly by the War Office in London, stating that he was required on 29 March 1915 to transfer to No 4 Squadron at St Omer in France, as an observer.

It was spring and the leaves were just appearing on the trees, hiding the squalor of the villages which were feeling the shock of war. The absence of young men and general feeling of dejection of a country close to the battlefield did not overshadow William's elation at his posting. St Omer was a hive of activity, no boredom here by all accounts, with aircraft being tested, repaired and flown to all parts of the war zone. The noise of engines revving and machine guns being tested. The place was alive with staff cars and activity, and with many types of flying machines in orderly rows. William could at last relate to this environment and threw himself into his new role with great enthusiasm. Within two weeks his Commanding Officer, Major C A Loncroft, confirmed his advancement to an 'efficient' observer, and increased his pay, much to William's delight.

It was in March 1915 that the Royal Flying Corps developed a new system of reporting the location of falling shells onto the target area – known as the 'clock code'. The target was the centre of an imaginary clock face with due north at 12 o'clock. Circles were drawn on the map around the target at varying distances from 10 to 500yds and were lettered, enabling the observer to call up the letter and distance on his morse key. A direct hit was tapped out as 'OK'. A simple but very effective method.

Flying the British Experimental 2C, William settled to the exacting role of air observer, learning the art of recording with accuracy the artillery positions and map reading from the air, as well as defending the aircraft when attacked by the enemy. In a letter home he wrote that he had at last found his goal – to fly!

His words to his mother:

Talking of beauty, you have no idea how beautiful it is above the clouds. I have been up at about 5 o'clock on a still afternoon – you have no idea how glorious it is to gaze at the earth 7000ft or over. But thrilling as it is, the real beauty comes with the clouds. Those rolling wastes of vapour of a hundred shades fading away 'til they terminate at the horizon into one straight line, or rather circle, which frames your view.' He went on to confirm: 'I love flying more and more every day, and the work is even more interesting than it was.'

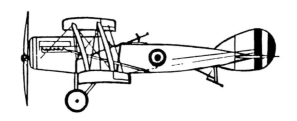

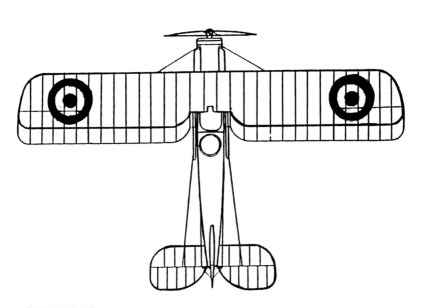

SPAN 39' 3"

LENGTH 25' 9"

PLAN No. 2

BRISTOL FIGHTER F2α (1917)

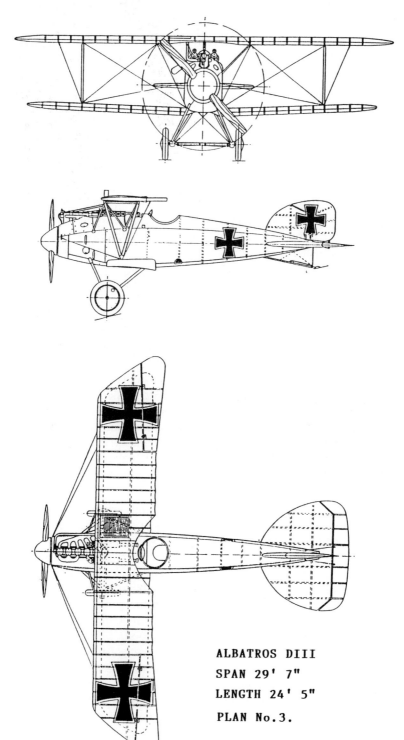

ALBATROS DIII
SPAN 29' 7"
LENGTH 24' 5"
PLAN No.3.

Leefe Robinson's routine meant artillery observation, methodically patrolling along the front lines, often distracted by the puffs of smoke of exploding anti-aircraft shells, noiseless in the distance; being deafened by the 90hp engine.

Two hundred BE2Cs were sent out to France during 1915 and No 4 Squadron received them in September to replace Moranes. Although flying machines were to be camouflaged later in the First World War, at this time the machines were clear doped all over, and it was not until April 1916 that orders were issued for BE2C squadrons in France to carry distinctive white or black bars and bands on the fuselage. These machines were the first British service aeroplanes to carry squadron markings.

Billy at last had found in his new environment an enthusiasm to excel at the adventure of being totally involved in a situation that not only excited him, but in which he felt he was making a positive contribution towards the job in hand. Assisting the artillery to pinpoint targets on the enemy positions, his reports, via his transmitter, gave the Battery Commander the map co-ordinates of the target, allowing the gunners to range onto the German gun emplacements. Simple directions to the ground by morse code soon ensured the target had been successfully destroyed. Accurate reading of the large, squared co-ordinates of the map taught William the importance of detailed, speedy analysis of often tricky situations. Observation of the flash from the muzzle of a field gun, or howitzer, which flung its deadly shells high in the air, needed sharp detection by the observer to pinpoint the location on a crumpled and well used map. Thankful that he was not crawling in the mud and devastation of the battlefield below, Billy constantly reminded himself of his good fortune at transferring from an army regiment to one of an aviator – often very cold and wet, but always with the dignity of being able to return to an airfield behind the front lines of the war zone.

He was billeted with a French peasant family – warm, homely people who idolised him as they would their own son. The hamlet still bore a resemblance to a quiet, tree-lined French village, showing no affluence, being a hard-working, farming community, where rural smells were part of every day existence. Billy wished he had paid more attention to his French studies in St Bees, as the limited vocabulary of his school days was barely enough to be understood, but with the genial hospitality of the village, he enjoyed acceptance into the family atmosphere he so longed for and which seemed just a memory of his boyhood.

He wrote home of the French boys in the towns selling newspapers and shouting out at the top of their voices in their strange accents – *Daily Mail*, *Daily Sketch*, and *The Times*, and of British Tommies arguing with the young boys over small transactions in the boulevards when buying their wares, or being directed to friendly girls who were pleased to make the

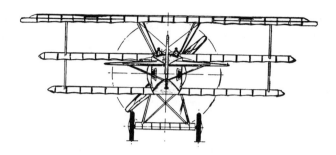

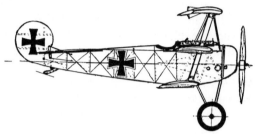

FOKKER Dr 1
SPAN 23' 7"
LENGTH 19' 0"
PLAN No.4.

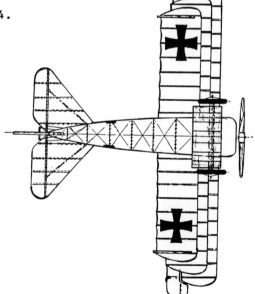

soldiers' stay a pleasant one, relaxing from the rigours of the nearby battlefields.

A background of gunfire gave an uncertain and unreal atmosphere to their lives – dawn patrols in the still, menacing light of a cold April morning – just one aircraft – pilot muffled in heavy topcoat, helmet and goggles – red-cheeked with vapoured breath – leather-gloved hands steady on the control stick, testing elevators on the tail plane – kicking the bar at his feet to check the rudder.

'Contact!' as the aircraftsman turned the propeller. 'Switch on!' The roar of the Renault engine, as the burst of power shook the airframe of the fuselage.

William Leefe Robinson settled into the front cockpit, aware of the strong smell of oil from a warming engine, going through the checklist with the pilot. The aircraft rumbled across the field through the clearing mist, the wind whistling in the bracing wires of the biplane's wings. With increased acceleration the pilot gently pulled the stick back, the tailplane lifting and, suddenly airborne, the spinning wheels silent as the 'plane rose into the air towards the bright flashes of distant explosions.

Men were standing in the trenches, facing an enemy equally alert to the potential agony of another day in the appalling conditions of a war-torn, devastated countryside which bore little resemblance to its beauty of yesteryear.

Over Cambrai the aircraft suddenly shook to the burst of shells from German anti-aircraft batteries. Shrapnel tore a jagged gap in the fabric of the starboard upper wing, too close to the main wooden strut for comfort! Billy instinctively ducked, and was annoyed with himself for not spotting the battery earlier, but at 5000ft they were an easy target. The noise of the black and white shell bursts was deafening. He turned round and smiled nervously, pursing his lips in disbelief at their good fortune in surviving almost a direct hit (although this was rarely achieved). Two hours later, cold and feeling miserable at the lack of success in obtaining any useful information, they came in low over the British lines and returned to the airfield, thankful to have survived yet another sortie over enemy lines.

Billy envied the single-seat fighter 'planes that flew purposefully over the salient, knowing the vulnerability of the BE2C as a sitting target for any German pilot who was determined enough to attack the aircraft. It was unusual for German machines to fly over the British lines and difficult to engage them in battle, as they declined combat if at all possible.

At this time the Dutchman, Anthony Fokker, who had been unable to impress the English Military Attachés in Berlin in 1912 with his potential as an aircraft designer, was perfecting not only German fighter 'planes, but synchronizing the firing of a machine gun forward through the propeller of an aircraft. An idea taken from the French pilot, Roland

Garros, whose attempts to fire a stream of lead bullets through the propeller of his single seat fighter had alarmed the German authorities. Unfortunately, the Frenchmen's secret weapon was soon discovered as, with a faulty engine, Garros had landed behind the enemy lines, revealing the secret and enabling Fokker to exploit the idea. Although Fokker had never handled a machine gun before, he adapted the German Parabellum machine gun within 48 hours and, in three days, had changed the course of aerial combat for all time.

It was not all routine patrols and severe disciplines of war for young Billy – known as 'Robbie' to his flying companions. At every opportunity he visited the town of St Omer and met the local girls who needed little encouragement to fall for his youthful and handsome looks. His charm and sense of fun set him apart from his companions who, in the uniform of the Royal Flying Corps, were greatly sought after by both matrons and mademoiselles.

It was ironic, perhaps even fortunate, that on 8 May 1915, Lt Leefe Robinson flew his last patrol as an observer because, wounded by shrapnel while flying a dawn reconnaissance, he was invalided back to England.

He wrote a letter to his mother from Clapham, London, on 14 May 1915:

It was about 4.50am on Saturday over Lille that the beasts got me – I thought I was bruised at first and went on with my reconnaissance, but after a bit my arm got a bit stiff and the blood dirtied all the maps, so we cut our reconnaissance short at the end and went back to the aerodrome. From there I went to the dressing hospital where they took out the shrapnel bullet and dressed the wound, and sent me off to Boulogne. I arrived there late on Saturday night and was told I should probably go to England – great was my joy!

William's aspirations to 'drive himself about' were freshened in his mind and he confided to Ruth, his sister, of his wish to become a pilot at the earliest opportunity.

Pre-flight discussion. William Leefe Robinson, Spring 1915
Mrs R. David

Rose and Daisy Jones 1917. Brooches show photos of William Bills,
Royal Engineers (Author's father) and Charlie Fry
Author's collection

5 English Rose

In the warm sunshine of England in May 1915, three young girls giggled and laughed as they scrambled excitedly up onto the seats of the pony and trap, and sat expectantly beside the bearded driver. Father cracked a long, corded whip in an endeavour to spark some enthusiasm into the beast for the long journey from Ilford to the rural, country outskirts of Romford in the county of Essex.

William Henry Jones, Builder and Decorator, was justly proud of his daughters – Daisy, serious and scholastic, just 19 years; Violet Victoria, two years younger, quiet, sitting shyly, knees firmly together, a litte unsure of herself; and the youngest, Rose, pretty as a picture, chattering with vivacity to the numerous boys clammering around the carriage. At 15 years of age, Rose was blossoming into an outstanding beauty, with large, doe-like eyes that melted young men with instincts to protect her. She tossed her head, the long dark tresses of her hair whipped into a frenzy of bubbling happiness.

The pony broke into a trot along the cobbled street with the boys running after them, trying to jump onto the running-step.

'Whip behind, Guv'nor!' the girls called in unison.

The wispy, alto-cumulus clouds set against a background of pale blue and grey sky, outlined the single aircraft on a routine flight from Hainault aerodrome to Suttons Farm at Hornchurch. A far cry from the appalling carnage of Flanders where thousands of young men were fighting in conditions quite beyond the comprehension of the girls.

Just a week earlier, the SS *Lusitania* had been sunk by a torpedo from a German 'U' boat in the Irish Sea with the loss of 1198 lives, including five babies.

The cottage on the outskirts of Romford nestled in an orchard of fruit trees, overlooked by farmland, and alongside ran a stream glistening in the bright sunlight. A haven from the Zeppelin raids along the East Coast of England. Bombs had been dropped at nearby Maldon in April that year, but such thoughts were far from Rosie's and Violet's minds that day, although Daisy's boyfriend, Charlie, was fighting in France with the Cycle Corps of The Essex Regiment.

The Jones family, c1915.
Back row, left to right. Daisy, Henry Jones (Father), Violet.
Front row, left to right. Rose, William, Annie Jones (Mother) née
Smeaton *Author's collection*

During the week, Daisy was employed as a 'bus conductress, taking fares on an open-topped vehicle as her contribution towards the war effort, thus relieving a man for active duty. She took great pride in her job and her uniform, complete with bush hat, turned up on one side New Zealand-fashion, making her a formidable opponent when the drunks tried to board the omnibus on Saturday nights. It was an entertainment for the locals to watch the policemen arresting rowdies as they were turned out of the 'pubs', usually after pay-day, when their hard-earned wages had been squandered before their womenfolk could get their hands on their meagre housekeeping allowances.

Rose worked at Fletchers, a printers, by the River Roding, not far from the clocktower at Ilford Broadway, a large, cobbled concourse diagrammatically criss-crossed with tram lines.

At that time Rose had no knowledge that her destiny was to meet and befriend an English Aviator known as William Leefe Robinson.

40

6 Billy the Birdman

Robinson reported at Farnborough on June 29 1915, and made his first flight under instruction the next day. On 18 July he made his first solo flight. Ten days later he qualified for the Royal Aero Club and was awarded Certificate No 1475, qualifying in a Maurice Farman 'Longhorn'. The Longhorn had a wing span of 50ft, giant skids projected in front, with four landing wheels. In the nacelle two seats allowed instructor and pupil to sit forward of the biplane wings, the tail and rudder being supported by four longerons, or tail booms, uncovered in fabric. In this quaint and ugly-looking machine, with its 70hp Renault engine, William qualified after only 3hrs 50mins' flying time. A further month of advanced training at the Central Flying School at Upavon then on 15 Septmber 1915, Lieutenant Leefe Robinson gained the coveted 'Wings', being designated a Flying Officer, and seconded to No 19 Squadron at Castle Bromwich, under the command of Capt R M Rodwell.

In Pollibetta, Co-org, in late October 1915, his mother received a long letter from her son:

You have just heard I have 'got my wings' – that is some time ago now. Ever since I have been here I've been acting as Flight Commander (a Captain's place) and second in command of the squadron. I have plenty to do with that alone, what with the five machines and about 35 men under me. I am also squadron photographer and wireless officer, added to which my machines are the only ones which carry machine guns, so they and their fittings have to be looked after. I'm going to give you an example of my abominable conceit. The other day it was most awfully windy and I was the only flying officer allowed to go up – I took a passenger too. What do you think of a pilot who pilots a machine and passenger through a 45mph gale!

Robinson excelled as a pilot, at last being at one with himself and his plane, enjoying every minute in the air – his confidence and ability unquestioned by his superiors. He delivered aircraft in October and November 1915, and letters home expressed his thoughts and aspirations:

You seem to think whenever I go to town or anywhere I must have leave – not at all. I go 'on duty'. I have delivered and brought machines to and from Farnborough, Northolt (Harrow) and various other places and between times I manage to have a peep at 'Town' and my various friends there. Whenever I do, I have a simply ripping time. I landed for lunch near Banbury the other day – you are immediately surrounded by people offering you cars, lunch, tea, bed and the Lord knows what not. Of course, if you are wise you generally pick out the grounds of a country house or large villa of some kind to land in. My last landing was at Kenilworth. I had a passenger with me and we had the time of our lives. Talk about autograph books and cameras. By gad, I was positively sick of seeing and signing my own signature. When I swore I would not sign another book one girl caught hold of my machine and said she would not leave until I signed. So after much amusing argument I told her to give me the book, whereupon I placed my filthy hand, writing 'The mark of an aviator, W L Robinson' over the top of the handmark – my hand was all dirty with the oil of the engine. The girl I liked best of all was a sweet little Flapper of about 17 called Kathleen Lennox for whom I drew our aeroplane. Another girl lent me her camera with which I took some photographs. She developed them and has just sent me some printed. We stayed at Kenilworth two days and a night!!

I have three observers and several flyers to instruct me in my flight. I take passengers up every day. Last Tuesday I was to take a passenger to Gosport (other side of the river to Portsmouth). We got as far as Oxford when the weather – wind, rain and fog – got so bad, that we had to land. We saw a machine already on Port Meadow, so I landed there too. The other machine turned out to be one which my best friend here was also taking to Gosport. To shorten a long story we had an A1 time in Oxford, got the local police and volunteers to guard the machines – put up at the Mitre Hotel – saw 'Déjà vu' at the theatre, and enjoyed ourselves generally. We were followed about most of the time by a band of small boys who would insist on cheering every now and then. Next morning the sky was perfect – and we decided to go on our way via Farnborough where we would fill up our petrol and oil tanks. I flew fairly high, touching nearly 9,000ft. As luck would have it my engine began missing. I knew exactly what the matter was but could not remedy it in the air. The poor observer, a fellow who had only been in an aeroplane about once before in his life, grew quite nervous, he kept on passing back notes to me: 'The front part of the machine is vibrating horribly' – 'What is the matter with the engine?' 'Will she hold out 'til we get to Farnborough?' etc. I laughed like anything at him, made a long nose and put my tongue out at him for a reply (you can't hear each other speak of course). Once or twice I held up my hands to show I wasn't holding anything – I thought the poor man would have a fit. Anybody who knew the least bit about flying would know we were as safe as a rock. I then shut off the engine and did a long glide of about six miles into Farnborough aerodrome.

On Christmas Eve 1915, Billy Robinson was lodging at the Lion Hotel, Farningham in Kent, being on loan to No 10 Reserve Squadron, one of the Home Defence units set up to protect London from the growing menace of Zeppelin raids. Throughout the year the Germans had systematically carried out raids on England, dropping 50lb bombs, and carrying over one hundred on each sortie. Although the frequency of the raids had subsided since October 1915, the Government's concern at the vulnerability of London to the raiders was paramount and they appointed

42

Sir Percy Scott to look at the gunnery defences of the capital. Previously, the Admiralty and the War Office had operated an unco-ordinated defence of London, using both army anti-aircraft artillery and those of naval units; neither authority accepting full responsibility for the defence of the city.

His mother received news in his usual 'chirpy' manner, and his letters advised her of his progress:

I've been 'lent' by my Birmingham Squadron to the London defence and here I am 18 miles east of the city and 5 miles out of Dartford, tucked away with another pilot, some mechanics and two aeroplanes for the purpose of 'Straffing Zepps' when they next come this way. The other pilot (who by the way was with me learning to fly at Farnborough) and myself are living in a sweet little country hotel, all on our own – we are awfully comfortable here and the job is really a very slack one. We are chosen for it because we are supposed to be able to fly by night, an accomplishment which not every pilot can boast of I may state. There are only 20 aeroplanes on the London defence, but we are absolutely the first to receive the enemy should they come over. Now for heaven's sake don't get nervous mother, the job is quite safe if one has plenty of confidence.

Leefe Robinson's commander was not at all happy with his secondment to a Home Defence Squadron, but his destiny was already predictable.

The year ended with a letter to his mother that gave his 'hearty wishes of luck and happiness throughout 1916 and all the following years, with love to all.' It was signed, 'I remain your ever loving son, Billy the Birdman.'

44

7 Night Fighter

In January 1916 Leefe Robinson delivered his last 'ferry' job, an Armstrong Whitworth FK3 from Newcastle to the Central Flying School at Upavon. Due to the weather conditions, he was unable to complete his assignment until 31 January, a night upon which the Midland Counties were raided by NINE ZEPPELINS. Bombs were dropped in Norfolk, Suffolk, Lincolnshire, Leicestershire, Derbyshire and Staffordshire. One airship, the L14, penetrated as far as Shrewsbury causing damage to Walsall and neighbouring towns. 70 persons were killed and 113 injured, of which 76 were women and 34 children. Eight defending aircraft crashed, and two of the pilots were killed.

The requirement for night-flying pilots became of paramount importance, and with great despatch William was sent to his first operational unit on 2 February 1916, assigned to Suttons Farm airfield, near Hornchurch in Essex, the future No 39 (Home Defence) Squadron, part of 19 Reserve Squadron under the command of Major T C Higgins.

The airfield formed part of the Manor of Suttons and the farmhouse was built on the site of the old Manor House, originally owned by William of Wykeham, in the year 1392. It was situated about a mile south of the church of Hornchurch, and was known to be one of the best airfields in England at that time. Strategically placed to defend London from the South and East, it shared its responsibilities with Hainault Farm Airfield to the North and North Weald Bassett to the North West.

39 Squadron was not fully operational in the early part of 1916, and it was not until April that three flights of BE2Cs, two at each of the airfields, were formed into a fighting unit for the defence of the capital.

Robinson recalls there were two 'night' fighters at the station and the aeroplanes were kept in large tents on the field. During lulls in operational flights the pilots were instructed to take up the machines at least twice a week to ensure they were fully operational and ready for use when called upon.

The Home Defence Squadron was gradually re-organised by Major Higgins and by July 1916 the squadron had grown to 18 aircraft, made up of three flights under the direction of Major A H Morton. Leefe Robinson was assigned 'B' Flight, with 'A' Flight led by Capt L S Rose and 'C' Flight by Lt Alfred de Bath Brandon, a New Zealander, at Hainault Farm airfield.

Initially, the BE2Cs were makeshift 'night' fighters, because their standard design had had to be modified for the job in hand. The normal observer's cockpit was 'faired' over and a locally-devised fixture was attached to the rear section of the upper wing at the centre section, on which a single Lewis machine gun was mounted to fire upwards. Spare drums of ammunition were carried in the pilot's cockpit and a Very-light pistol for signalling. Although the pilot could, generally, detect road networks, rivers and railway lines from the air on a moonlit night, the problem of landing in the dark was an ever present hazard. Landing flares were lit on the airfield in the form of an 'L' shape and, at about 500ft a Very-light curving in a red ball into the darkness would warn the ground staff of the pilot's wish to land, whereupon an answer was given by Very-light fired from the ground, confirming all was clear. (Eventually, Holt Flares were fixed under the aircraft's lower wings to aid night landings.) The essential night flying instruments were eventually illuminated and the figures and 'hands' of the dials marked with radium, luminous paint. Landing was the most difficult of the pilots problems and many were killed returning to the airfields from a 'Zepp' straffing job – as they called such operations. Lighting of the runways at night consisted of paraffin-soaked rags in tin barrels, spaced each side of the runway.

A great camaraderie existed in William's 'B' Flight, which comprised Lts Brock, Durston, Mallinson, Frederick Sowrey and W J Tempest, all of whom became great friends, enjoying not only their official duties but, when off-duty, the adulation of the female company in the nearby towns of Romford and Ilford.

On 26 February 1916, however, Billy lost his brother-in-law and cousin, Arthur Robinson, who had died in France on active service from wounds received in battle. After marrying Grace Leefe Robinson in 1913, they worked in West Africa and then he joined the Northamptonshire Regiment. Billy always referred to his sister as 'G', and wrote to her expressing his sorrow:

My darling girl, I wish I had sufficient power of expression to comfort you in the minutest degree. He is a loss – a greater loss than I can express – to all who knew him, but my dear girl one is bound to gain some consolation in knowing that one of the finest men on God's earth has met with the finest end that a man can possibly hope for.

In the spring of 1916 Zeppelin raids continued to harass the population, often with devastating effect, killing many civilians and maiming others. In March, five German airships raided Lincolnshire, Essex and Suffolk, and their bombs killed 48 persons, including 31 soldiers of the 3rd Manchesters, who were billeted in a chapel in Cleethorpes. Of the five raiders, two were damaged by gunfire near Stowmarket, but managed to get back to their home base. An L15 was compelled to land in the Thames Estuary, where the crew surrendered to the Captain of HMS *Olivine*. The naval craft took the Zeppelin in tow, but it sank soon afterwards. The raids persisted and 'B' Flight began to get impatient at their lack of success in finding the enemy – who managed to avoid all their efforts at contact.

On 25 April at 10.45pm, with orders to patrol at 5,000ft, Leefe Robinson steadily climbed in his flimsy BE2C until his altimeter read 7,000ft. The searchlights in the distance were pointing towards the north when, suddenly, above him he saw the enormous shape of a Zeppelin. With pulses racing he slowly climbed towards the gigantic airship until the monster was just 2,000ft above him. Positioning his machine under the Zeppelin he fired burst after burst of bullets from his Lewis machine gun. Five times the gun jammed, and the bullets appeared to have little effect on the monster above him, although he saw a flash of light in the forward gondola. With only twenty bullets spent he cursed the gun's lack of support at the crucial moment, losing the Zeppelin as it sped off, rising easily into the clouds in an E.N.E. direction. Billy tried to follow but soon lost sight of the 'Zepp' and returned to his patrol. In the distance he could see the ground flares of Suttons Farm and lights along the length of the River Thames, easily distinguished from the air by an enemy. He thought – '. . . how foolish to light the route to the capital!' Five miles north-east of Suttons Farm he could see a light signalling – a spy perhaps – five fast flashes then a pause followed by another five flashes. He reported this on landing at 1.15am, and commented on Hainault Farm airfield's confusion of ground flares with no base to the 'L' shape – so necessary to indicate to the pilot the direction into which he was to land.

April 1916 brought bad news for Billy of his brother, Harold, who had been badly wounded in Mesopotamia. Harold had joined the 101st Grenadiers of the Indian Army and was attached to the 103rd when a British attempt to relieve Kut-el-Amara failed, resulting in many casualties; and later the surrender of General Townsend with 9,000 British and Indian troops after a siege of 143 days. Harold died of his wounds on 10 April 1916.

In the summer of 1916, albeit one where the weather left much to be desired, the German raiders were conspicuous by their absence, due partly to atrocious weather conditions and short nights.

With time on their hands Leefe Robinson, Fred Sowrey and William Tempest had every opportunity to discuss at length the news of the day. The Battle of Jutland, known to the Germans as the Battle of Skagerrak, and the British warships' attack under the command of Admiral Jellicoe soon after the German Fleet had put to sea on 30 May 1916.

The two great powers had formed a mighty array of armoured ships: Dreadnoughts; Battle Cruisers, and Destroyers. The ensuing battle was fought fiercely by both antagonists, with the loss by the British of three Battle Cruisers – *Invincible, Indefatigable* and *Queen Mary*: Three Cruisers – *Black Prince, Defence* and *Warrior*, and eight Destroyers – *Ardent, Fortune, Nestor, Nomad, Shark, Sparrowhawk, Tipperary* and *Turbulent*. The Germans lost one Battleship – the *Pommern*; the Battle Cruiser – *Lutzow*; four light Cruisers – *Elbing, Frauencob, Rostock* and *Wiesbaden*, and five Destroyers. Over 328 British officers and 5,769 ratings were killed, and 160 officers of the German Fleet, and 2,385 men were killed.

The British Government's policy of building fast, heavily-armed but lightly-armoured ships had not paid off against that of the German Fleet, whose designers had preferred to sacrifice speed and gun power in favour of heavy armour plating and armour piercing shells.

Billy and his colleagues continually talked of problems with their own aircrafts' armament and their inability to bring the huge Zeppelins down by machine-gun fire. It was a relief when they heard of an Australian Engineer, John Pommeroy, and his new design of an explosive bullet which, used in combination with a bullet invented by Commander Frederick Brock, was to prove most effective in the months ahead. The Royal Flying Corps immediately ordered large stocks of the new ammunition, with drums of the new bullets for the Lewis guns. Used with the Buckingham incendiary bullet this was to prove deadly for the Zeppelin.

It was not until 28 July that the new, super Zeppelin was again seen over Britain, when ten airships attacked the coastal towns, fortunately with little damage. Only one ship, an old type L13, penetrated the defences just south of the River Humber. The Zeppelins flew at enormous heights dropping bombs indiscriminately, without any effective plan and a further three attacks in August showed little effort on the part of the Zeppelin Commanders. They did no serious damage, except in Hull, on the night of the 8 August, when 10 persons were killed and a number injured. The anti-aircraft defences around London had improved under the leadership of Sir Percy Scott, forcing the enemy aircraft to such heights that the dropping of bombs with any accuracy became impossible.

The people of Hornchurch, near Suttons Farm airfield, were very conscious of the defence of the country by the intrepid flyers 'down the road' and the activities at the field were a constant source of admiration by the villagers. The flyers were well aware of the hero-worship, particularly by the young ladies of the district, and no finer exhibitions of flying were seen to promote that excitement. The flyers also attended civic functions during lulls in the fighting, and Billy Robinson would call on the young boys of the Cottage Homes (of the parish of St Leonard, Shoreditch) at the model village in Hornchurch Road (between the village and Romford), or offer his thanks to the little girls of the Queen Mary's Needlework Guild who turned out numerous knitted garments – socks, helmets and scarves – for the soldiers and airmen who were faced with the oncoming winter under canvas. Generally, the population came out at night to watch the flyers take off in the dark and climb up to reach the enemy aircraft – it was awe-inspiring to see the biplanes take off in the light of the many flares lining the runway – the roar of the engines as the twilight faded and moonlight – 'Zepp weather' – lit up the cloud formation, swept by brilliant searchlight beams criss-crossing in their search of the elusive airships. Unmistakable when found! Brilliant, silver, cigar-shaped monsters that appeared and disappeared, ascending rapidly into the darkness of cloud cover – the occasional whistle of a 50lb bomb and *crump* as it explodes in a field, or a blinding flash as the explosion rips through a building – falling masonry, clouds of dust, then silence – a cry – a dog barks, feverish activity to release those trapped in the debris, the clang of a fire-tender bell – the smell of saturated, wet and burnt wood in your nostrils – the stupidity of it – the blessing it was over there and not here! The folks of Hornchurch knew these feelings and were glad they had their own defenders close to hand, grateful in many ways.

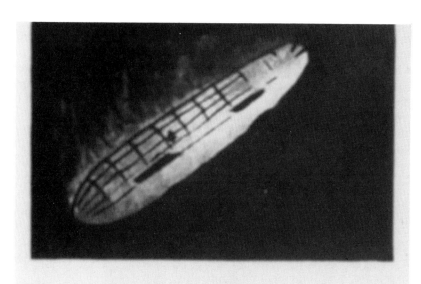

In Never Loving
Memory Of
— L21 —

(Fell at Cuffley Sept. 3rd 1916)

THIS IS THE FATE OF A BOMB DROPPING ZEP
WHICH VISITED ENGLAND WHILST CIVILIANS SLEPT
THEY LITTLE THOUGHT THEIR TIME SO SHORT
TILL IN FLAMES TO EARTH 'TWAS QUICKLY BROUGHT
DEATH CLAIMED EACH ONE ERE THEY COULD PRAY
HAVE MERCY LORD ON US THIS DAY.

8 Count von Zeppelin

In the year 1784 the first dirigible balloon took to the air, invented by the brothers Robert, being the beginnings of the enormous, rigid airships. It was fish-shaped and had a double envelope, so paving the way for the system used with later airships of the type designed by Count von Zeppelin. The first aluminium, motor-driven, dirigible airship was built by Ferdinand von Zeppelin in 1900. He had become interested in balloons whilst serving with the German Volunteer Corps, on the Union side, during the American Civil War; later serving with a squadron of Würtemberg Cavalry. By 1885 he had retired from the Cavalry, although his interest in ballooning had persisted, and he made application to the King of Würtemberg for financial aid to pursue and perfect his inventions. The first Zeppelin was 420ft long, with an aluminum framework and a car carrying two 16hp Daimler motors. It resembled a gigantic cigar and managed to fly a few miles, very slowly, before descending onto Lake Constance, where it was accommodated in a mammoth, floating hangar. Five years later his second airship (slightly smaller, but with more powerful 170hp engines) was wrecked in a gale. A successful, third attempt produced a Zeppelin capable of travelling at 30mph and could accommodate 11 passengers. The airship was named 'Zeppelin I' and was purchased by the German Government as part of a War Fleet. His fourth creation was wrecked, and destroyed by fire, following a bad landing, shortly after losing the Lake Constance hangar in a storm. The Kaiser became a patron of the venture and with a public subscription of over £300,000, the Count was proclaimed the greatest German of the 20th century and awarded the Prussian Order of Merit, a most coveted and distinguished Order of that time.

In 1910 the German Zeppelin Company produced its first passenger airship, the *Deutschland* but this, too, was wrecked shortly afterwards. Undaunted, the idea of a vast, rigid airship inspired von Zeppelin to produce others, each with various improvements on its predecessor. Zeppelin knew large airships had great military potential, being able to ascend quickly to considerable heights without the necessity of carrying large amounts of fuel. His first Zeppelin had a balloon capacity of 400,000 cubic feet, holding 16 gas containers. The massive, lattice framework was

SHUTTE LANZ SL11
570Ft. LENGTH.
 66Ft. DIAMETER.
FOUR ENGINES: 960 H.P.

R.A.F. B.E.2c (No.2693).
27'-3" LENGTH.
37'-0" WING SPAN.

ALTITUDE 11,500 FT.

THE BATTLE

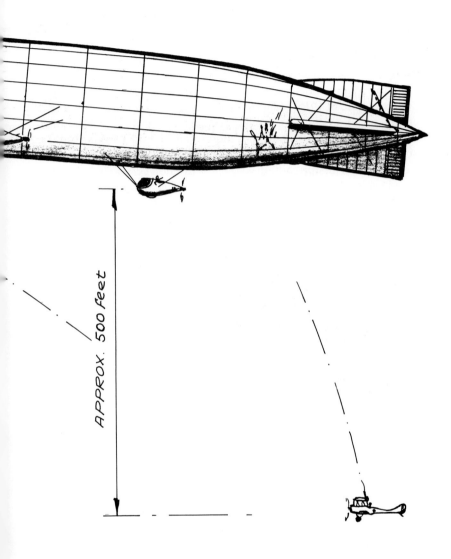

APPROX. 500 Feet

Author's Impression

filled with hydrogen gas and covered with linen and silk – all very inflammable. Other German designers produced similar structures. The Schutte-Lanz Company produced rigid airships on a wooden framework, which were built at Leipzig.

With the onset of war, the German High Command quickly saw the potential of the airship for naval duties in an observation role, and for use by the army to carry bombs. The acknowledged leader of airships was Fregattenkapitan Peter Strasser, who considered it his duty to bring England to her knees with continual attacks on the mainland. One of his most brilliant commanders was Kapitan Mathy, who flew many sorties over England. Late in 1915, Hauptmann Wilhelm Emil Ludwig Schramm took command of a Schutte-Lanz SL11, a new ship which entered into service on 12 August 1916, and had attempted to raid England on 31 August, but had been turned back by bad weather conditions. Schramm was an experienced airship captain who knew London very well, being the son of the London representative of the Siemens Electrical Company. He had been born at Old Charlton in Kent, and lived in England until he was 15 years old, returning to Germany on the death of his father. He had flown on several raids in airships, including the Zeppelin LZ39 and on taking up his command of the SL11, had marshalled an experienced crew of fifteen men – who also had a destiny with 'Billy the Birdman'.

9 Zeppelin Raid

On the morning of 2 September 1916, sixteen airships, twelve from the German Naval Airship Division and four from the Army Division, were being prepared for the first combined operation by the German forces for a large-scale raid on England and the capital. Hauptmann Schramm mustered his 15-man crew of gunners, 'bomb' man and machinists, instructing Oberleutnant Vohdin to ensure that the ammunition, bombs and guns were stored satisfactorily. The weather was clear and the night promised to meet all the needs of the operation. The gondola of the airship resembled the bridge of a battleship in many ways and in his cramped quarters the Commander set course for England in the twilight of the evening, crossing the coast at Foulness Point at 10.40pm and approaching London in a wide sweep over Essex into Hertfordshire.

At Suttons Farm airfield, Lt Leefe Robinson and Lt Fred Sowrey sat in their BE2C aircraft, the engines warming up, in anticipation of their 'search and find' operation, now a routine with which they were both familiar. At 11.08pm the machines rose swiftly into the misty night air, the airstream cooling William's face as he climbed steadily over the next hour to 10,000ft. With instructions to patrol between the airfield and Joyce Green, he settled to his allotted 'beat', keeping a sharp look-out for Huns. The night aloft was beautifully clear and he counted ten sets of flares in the distance, but no enemy aircraft. With the River Thames a luminous guide to the capital, he had little difficulty keeping to the route of his designated patrol. Naval and Light ships in the North Sea were busy sending warnings of the approaching air armada to the Home Defence Headquarters at Horseguards, Whitehall. The anti-aircraft gunners in Hyde Park, primed and prepared for the anticipated attack, rested uneasily in the silence of the night. The citizens of London had put their children to bed, and few were concerned at the possibility of yet another raid, so set about retiring for the night.

In the early hours of 3 September, the first bombs fell on London Colney, North Mimms and North East London. Schramm had approached the capital over Royston and Hitchin, and commenced to release the deadly 50lb bombs, causing considerable damage.

Leefe Robinson had seen little evidence of the enemy as he patrolled, until 1.10am, two hours after leaving the airfield, he caught sight of a Zeppelin in the crossed beams of two searchlights over Woolwich. The clouds had collected in this quarter and the searchlight crews had difficulty keeping the airships in the shafts of brilliant light. Londoners were soon alerted to the drama and, despite the bombing, poured out onto the streets to gaze up into the night sky. Robbie, in BE2C 2963, checked his three drums of Brock and Pommeroy ammunition, wondering where the other pilots were flying in the darkness – Freddy could not be far away, and at least nine other machines were airborne. (Unknown to Billy, Freddy Sowrey had been forced to return to Suttons Farm 2 hours earlier due to engine failure.)

Far below, in the darkened streets of Ilford, by the Post Office in Clements Road, the Jones family stood, shawls wrapped around the girls – Rose, holding her younger brother William's hand, gazed in awe at the great silver mass caught in the glare of the searchlights. Oblivious of the drama, little Lilian Scott of Harold Weald slept in her bed whilst her parents stood in the garden, spellbound, as the giant airship fought to get out of the web of light to escape to the cover of the thickening clouds.

The Zeppelin LZ98, under the command of Hauptmann Ernst Lehmann, was caught in the light and the airship shook to the explosions of anti-aircraft fire from the batteries at Dartford and Tilbury. The commander had dropped bombs over an area he believed to be the London Docks. Lehmann ascended to 13,000ft, with the tiny fighter in pursuit. Slowly Robinson gained on his prey, avoiding the searching beams of light to surprise the ship from above but, just as he had positioned the BE2C for an attack, the Zeppelin disappeared into thick cloud. The experienced Lehmann ascended rapidly, after jettisoning water ballast and his remaining bombs to lighten the airship. Disappointed, Lt Leefe Robinson turned away to resume his patrol, aware of his lack of fuel and his restricted flying time.

Over Finsbury and Victoria Park the searchlights had caught the huge Schutte-Lanz SL11 in powerful beams of light, and the ship was surrounded by explosions from anti-aircraft shells, without any apparent effect on this immense invader. The Zeppelin was travelling at top speed, diving then ascending, throwing out tremendous clouds of black smoke which completely hid it from view. Ascending quickly to avoid the tremendous efforts of the gunners to bring the ship down, Schramm calmly issued instructions to his crew.

Completely heedless of his low fuel supply, on sighting the SL11, Leefe Robinson fearlessly gave chase and was joined by 2/LT Mackay and 2/Lt Hunt – all experienced night fighters – tiny protagonists determined to do

56

Robinson seated in BE2c 2963 after the attack on SL 11. This aircraft
was destroyed by fire on 16 Sept 1916   *Christie's*

battle with the enemy. Hauptmann Schramm, a serious disciplinarian,
jettisoned his remaining bombs to lighten his craft.

Two little sisters, hand-in-hand, in a field watched the huge Zeppelin in
its death throes as it tried in vain to avoid the attention of the defenders. A
50lb bomb whistled down and, in a blinding flash, the elder girl was dead
and the other lay dying!

The crowd below gasped as the ship was lost in the clouds, but cheered
as it re-appeared with shells bursting around the enormous, fabric-
covered hull – most of them too high or too low, with tracer bullets arching
over the ship. They saw one tiny fighter plane speedily overtaking its
colossal adversary and, within seconds, Leefe Robinson had raked the
underside of the ship with one drum from his Lewis machine gun. The
crowd fell silent, as did the guns, in deference to Goliath's attacker.
Robinson was surprised that the Brock and Pommeroy incendiary bullets
had failed to affect the ship in any way, and swiftly avoided the menacing
flashes of return fire from the airship's gondola.

Bombs had rained down on the towns of Edmonton and Ponders End,
destroying buildings in Turkey Street, but undaunted, the Londoners
continued to watch the spectacle unfolding before them of the destruction
of the hated Zeppelin. Sixteen persons had been killed during the attack.

PUBLIC WARNING

The public are advised to familiarise themselves with the appearance of British and German Airships and Aeroplanes, so that they may not be alarmed by British aircraft, and may take shelter if German aircraft appear. **Should hostile aircraft be seen,** take shelter **immediately** in the nearest available house, preferably in the basement, and remain there until the aircraft have left the vicinity: do not stand about in crowds **and do not touch unexploded bombs.**

In the event of **HOSTILE** aircraft being seen in country districts, the nearest Naval, Military or Police Authorities should, if possible, be advised immediately by Telephone of the TIME OF APPEARANCE, the DIRECTION OF FLIGHT, and whether the aircraft is an Airship or an Aeroplane.

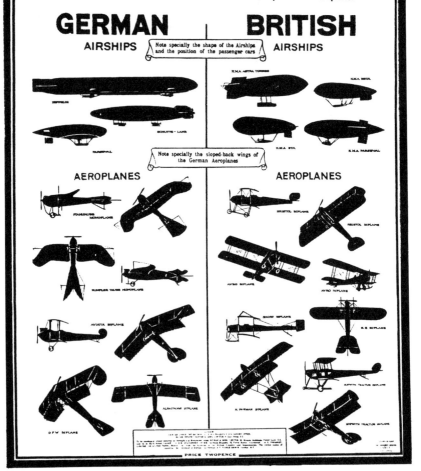

GERMAN | BRITISH

AIRSHIPS | AIRSHIPS

Note specially the shape of the Airships and the position of the passenger cars

Note specially the sloped-back wings of the German Aeroplanes

AEROPLANES | AEROPLANES

PRICE TWOPENCE

Billy Robinson pressed home his attack and flying alongside at 11,500ft, fired another drum of bullets, raking the ship from end to end without any apparent effect. He turned the fighter to approach from the rear, some 500ft below, and pumped his last drum into the belly of the giant between its twin rudders. Suddenly, he saw a glow of red light appear on the airship that grew within seconds into a blazing inferno! He banked away quickly to avoid the intense heat as the fabric of this massive ship began to disintegrate, the hydrogen gas igniting it into a scorching fire-ball.

Six-year-old Lily, the eldest of three children sheltering under the table in a small house in Leytonstone, was dragged out by her father, still clutching her brother. 'Quickly, the "Zepp" is coming down!' he yelled. Mother scrambled out from under the stairs, clasping her baby girl to her breast as they rushed out into the street to see the fiercely burning airship turn up its tail into a vast burning 'V'-shaped coffin. It hung for seconds, suspended by a vacuum, illuminating the whole of London. The population went crazy – cheering and clapping in a mad frenzy of relief. All of London appeared to be cheering so loudly it sounded like the roar of the crowd in a Football Stadium at the winning goal!

Ray, a young boy in Bush Hill Park, Enfield, saw Robinson's red Very-light soar up into the air in his jubilation, and felt a tremendous sense of pride in the victory over the enemy airship. The ship fell in one huge, tangled mass of burning debris, one of the propellers from its engines flying off from the wreckage and, with fragments falling from the doomed ship, it crashed into a field in the village of Cuffley, Hertfordshire, opposite the Plough Inn.

At Ilford, the population shouted and clapped, as did young Rosie Jones, who was promptly castigated by her mother, Annie, and told to consider the feelings of the mothers whose sons were dying in the airship; concluding firmly with the futility of fighting and loss of young men who were perishing in the blazing inferno. Feelings were mixed but, in general, Londoners were elated at the victory, knowing the effect it would have on the German aviators that, after all, the Zeppelin was not invincible.

Trains were toot-tooting their hooters as the 'spark' hit the 'Zepp' from above and it suddenly caught fire.

Excitement in the home of Henry Workman in Leytonstone kept the whole family, including his daughter Marjorie, in anticipatory suspense at the prospect of him travelling through the night with his brother, Ben, to see the blazing wreckage, as they hurriedly prepared for the journey to Cuffley.

Robbie fired off a few more Very-lights and a parachute flare, in his elation, but knowing his fuel and oil tanks were almost empty, returned to Suttons Farm, landing at 2.45am, his wheels touching down alongside the paraffin-can flares, and rolling gradually to a stop at the final illuminated marker. Fitters rushed over to steady the aircraft into its storage bay, and were amazed to see that he had shot away part of the central topwing and the machine-gun wire guard, luckily without collapsing from the top wings. Leefe Robinson had returned from a most hazardous sortie with petrol all but exhausted, in a badly damaged aircraft, landing in conditions where the ground visibility was not good. A few more minutes in the air would have proved disastrous.

Tired and weary, Billy lifted himself out of the cockpit, to be greeted by ecstatic ground crews who cheered and congratulated him . . . 'Well done, Sir!' . . . 'Good ol' Robbie – that'll show the blighters!' They lifted him shoulder high and carried him to the Flight Office to report his victory. Meantime, Lt Fred Sowrey, who had returned earlier, joined in the celebrations. The two pilots were both satisfied with the night's work as they wrote their patrol reports for the Officer Commanding No 39 Home Defence Squadron. A night which was to be remembered for the rest of the 20th century and known as 'Zepp Sunday'.

10 Zepp Sunday

A considerable number of the people of London had seen the greatest spectacle since the Fire of London some 250 years previously, and adrenalin coursed through the veins of the many who had witnessed the destruction, by fire, of the first Zeppelin to be brought down over Great Britain. Regardless of falling shrapnel from anti-aircraft shells and exploding bombs, Londoners and others from around the capital, danced in the streets, hooted hooters, rang bells and, generally, created such a din that it was impossible to sleep. The excitement spread like the fire that had vanquished the foe. The great feeling of relief felt by the majority of the populace incensed them to behave in a manner more befitting to the 'bullring', and they revelled in the total destruction of both men and monster that had wrought so much havoc on their homes and city.

A 17-year-old girl at Upminster, however, who saw the 'spark' hit the Schutte-Lanz and witnessed the fire spreading through the stricken ship, cried at the thoughts of the men burning to death, and clamped her hands over her ears to cut out the noise of the people cheering. The shrill toot-tooting of nearby railway engines deafened her, as the excited drivers frantically jerked the lanyard up and down, and hung out of their cabs to get a better view of the disaster.

As the Klaxon siren wailed its message that the raid was over, a great movement of Londoners stirred in the dimly lit streets. Bicycles appeared with hastily clad riders, caps askew and scarves flying, who raced through the night.

13-year-old Marjorie, living in Leytonstone, near Wanstead Flats, stood in awe as the dull, orange, looming mass of tangled debris settled slowly down from the sky, brightly illuminating the silhouetted houses. She tugged excitedly at her father's jacket sleeve as he and his brother, Benjamin, hurriedly grabbed their top coats. With a brief goodbye to the family, they rushed out into the night to walk to the scene of the crashed derigible.

Ray's father, in Bush Hill Park, Enfield, swung the starting handle of his 'Globe' automobile breathlessly and, bundling the boy into the car, with mounting excitement sped off to join the crowds en route to the burning wreckage.

Lt Frederick Sowrey, DSO and Lt William Leefe Robinson VC,
c1916.   *Mrs R. David*

Three Zeppelin wreckers. Lt Tempest, DSO; Lt Robinson, VC; Lt
Sowrey, DSO   *Rotary Photo*

Thora Edwards, in Plaistow, just six years old, hid behind her mother's skirt, her large eyes reflecting the brilliant light of the dying airship, as she saw a black object fall from the midships gondola, watching it tumble earthwards to disappear behind the backcloth of buildings.

The stricken ship took a long time to come down, gradually changing its shape into a 'V' and, finally, breaking into two sections and crashing onto a field. Great clouds of sparks and flaming debris were thrown up, to the cries of 'Hurrah for England', and 'This will be a lesson to the baby murderers.'

The army moved in quickly to put a cordon around the burning wreckage, but not before many souvenirs had been taken illegally by the enthusiastic crowd, who had come from many parts of the Home Counties to gloat over the fallen antagonist. The charred bodies of the 16 airmen lay scattered in the debris. The Commander lay on his back, the top half of his body resplendent in his high buttoned tunic, the lower half charred beyond recognition; an airman who had died for his fatherland.

The War Office was quick to exploit the situation of the destruction of the 'Zepp', albeit that it was a wooden framework Schutte-Lanz, and not the aluminium framework structure of a Zeppelin. Lord French issued an official despatch:

The large amount of wood employed in the framework is startling, and would seem to point to a shortage of aluminium in Germany.

The public were not really concerned at the details of the Government's propaganda and morale over the whole country took a great boost.

As the wreckage, which burned for two days, cooled, various sections survived total destruction: the control gondola; four burned engines; a thermos flask; a ceremonial sword; a revolver; three iron crosses; a gold cross; a clock (which had stopped at 03.10hrs) and a pair of cuff-links, picked up from the skeleton of the airship by young Ray and his father. The charred pages of a bible were lifted out of the charcoal remains – vanquished and victor sought solace in the same God.

The people of Hornchurch soon realised the hero who had destroyed the 'Zepp' was from their own airfield, and felt extreme satisfaction with the airman who had carried out such a feat. They planned to celebrate in their own manner in his honour. One eye-witness described the event:

With many of our neighbours I had the unique experience of seeing the first Zeppelin brought down in flames. We had been watching the gun flashes and searchlights, which had by now (2.00am) receded in a north-westerly direction, when suddenly we saw a red flare light floating in the sky; gun fire had ceased and then in a few moments the whole neighbourhood was brilliantly lit up, and to our great delight and wonderment we saw the Zeppelin falling down in flames. We could hardly believe the evidence of our eyes, our wonder was so great, but our delight was intensified when we learned a little later that Lt Robinson, from our own aerodrome, was the plucky aviator who had accomplished the gallant deed.

Alice Delysia, 1916. 'With all my heart I am thinking of you Dear
Captain Robinson'   *Christie's*

Special excursion trains were immediately organised by the railway company and over 10,000 persons were to travel from Kings Cross to the tiny village of Cuffley over two days. Extra police and army personnel augmented the already hard-pressed military guards around the wreck. The field soon became a quagmire and tempers became frayed as the crowds pushed forward to get a better and, in some cases, macabre view of the fallen ship. The roads around the village became impassable with carts and motor cars blocking the routes. Traders soon realised the sales potential of the event, and souvenirs, cards and photographs of both the airman and the airship falling from the skies, were soon available. Food quickly ran out at the Plough Inn and thirsts remained unquenched.

After a few hours' sleep, Billy Robinson and a number of fellow officers travelled to Cuffley to view the wreckage, where he was immediately mobbed by the enthusiastic crowd, who left him in little doubt of their worship for a hero.

On 6 September, the bodies of the German crew were buried at Hutton Lane Cemetery, Potters Bar Corner, but not before some of the crowd had thrown eggs at the coffins. Members of the Royal Flying Corps carried the wooden caskets shoulder high to a mass grave, dug quickly for the occasion. Hundreds watched the burial, many unhappy at the simple ceremony and, with mixed feelings, they stood in groups as the uncapped servicemen solemnly carried out the gruesome task of the burial of the enemy in an English field.

On the same day, 16-year-old Frances Bamford was buried with her 12-year-old sister Eleanor, fatally injured by a bomb from the SL11. The two sisters, daughters of the local blacksmith, had been struck down alongside the village church, which had been severely damaged.

Lt-Col Holt sent a brief report from Adastral House to Field Marshal Lord French:

Herewith report by Lt W L Robinson of his attack against the hostile airship this morning; a full 'operations summary' will be forwarded as soon as the other reports have been received. Six pilots were sent up around London and others in Kent and Yorkshire. There were no casualties to pilots, two machines were wrecked. Operations were interfered with by fog in some districts.

Lt Robinson has done good night work against Zeppelins during previous raids. It is very important that the successful method of attack remains secret, and instructions have, therefore, been issued that the public are to be told that the attack was made by incendiary bombs from above.

Later, Maj-Gen W Shaw memo-ed Lt-Gen Henderson, Commander of the Royal Flying Corps, on Lord French's behalf.

The Field Marshal Commanding-in-Chief has seen the attached reports, and will be glad to know if you have any recommendation to make with regard to any reward which you may consider the Officer concerned may be deserving of. He will be glad of an early reply.

Henderson's reply was immediate.

I recommend Lt W L Robinson for the Victoria Cross for the most conspicuous gallantry displayed in this successful attack.

On 5 September 1916, the *London Gazette* announced:

War Office, 5th September, 1916. His Majesty the King has been graciously pleased to award the Victoria Cross to the undermentioned officer:

Lieutenant William Leefe Robinson, Worcestershire Regiment and Royal Flying Corps. For most conspicuous bravery. He attacked an enemy airship under circumstances of great difficulty and danger, and sent it crashing to the ground as a flaming wreck. He had been in the air for more than two hours and had previously attacked another airship during his flight.

The newspapers spread the story of the victory throughout the land and the reaction of the public to the news was unpredictable – a hysteria swept through the towns and villages at Leefe Robinson's success. Billy found it impossible to travel about the countryside without being accosted by well-wishers. Within days, letters and telegrams arrived congratulating him on his success, some of the letters contained money to wish him good fortune.

The proprietor of the *Newcastle Daily Chronicle*, Col Joseph Cowen, presented Robinson with £2,000. William Bow, a Paisley shipbuilder, and a Mr L A Oldfield each gave £500. Lord Michelham, of the Bankers Herbert Stern, contributed £1,000. Gifts of £100 were received from Messrs G Wigley and J Ball and a gold watch from members of the Overseas Club. One young lady, just 18 years of age, wrote:

I wish I were so brave and did so much good. I have 15 different buttons on my coat from my soldier friends, also an RFC badge which I shall wear with more pleasure. I send you my love and big kiss of thanks. I shall be delighted to receive a card from you – Florence Label David.

He received over £4,200 and was overwhelmed by the response from the public.

Robbie's 'I only did my job . . .' was the disarmingly modest, hero's response to his admirers – not the least of whom were the airfield crews, who thought very highly of him as an officer, and who was often seen working with them like a mechanic. He had never had so much money and, as the invitations rolled in from all over the country to attend functions and dinners, he could not believe his good luck. His first purchase was a 'Prince Henry' Vauxhall automobile, and he and Freddy readily accepted many invitations.

Billy Robinson's handsome features, lithe figure and smart appearance made him a very attractive proposition for the adoring female population of Hornchurch, and his fame spread quickly to the rest of the country.

Reverse of Robinson's VC   *Christie's*

The French actress, Alice Delysia, a dancer with the Folies Bergère and Moulin Rouge in Paris, fell in love with him and wrote letters of adulation, but Billy just grinned, happy at his new found success; his pleasant manner and quiet demeanour overcoming any desire to let the success go to his head.

On 6 September 1916, the church bells were rung, rejoicing at the shooting down of the Schutte-Lanz SL11 by Lt Robinson and the folks of Hornchurch gave thanks for a great victory.

On 8 September, he was summoned to attend a special investiture by King George V at Windsor Castle, where crowds had gathered to welcome the hero. This modest, quiet man was amazed to see so many people, who cheered him loudly as the motor car hurried him to the Castle. At Runnymede, much to his horror, the car broke down, and the royal carriage which had been stationed at Windsor railway station, left without him, assuming he had been unable to attend the investiture. In a fearful fright at the thought of keeping his Sovereign waiting, he and a fellow officer eventually motored into the palace yard. The King affixed the Victoria Cross to his tunic, warmly congratulating him on his gallant feat, then proceeded to interrogate the intrepid airman on the action of bringing down the Zeppelin. They spent some time looking at photographs of the battlefront in Flanders, which had been sent to the King by the Prince of Wales. Impressed by the King's obvious admiration for both English and French aviators, he surprised Billy further by asking after his father and grandfather, William Braham Robinson, who had been Chief Constructor at Portsmouth Dockyard. Queen Mary showed equal interest and asked many questions, as did Prince Albert.

Billy had felt great apprehension at meeting the King, only to be put very much at his ease, and he was more embarrassed to hear the accolade from the huge crowd outside the Castle, who cheered and shouted as they eagerly lined the streets. A great warmth of hero worship and gaiety took over the town – the like of which the townsfolk had not seen for many a year – as Lt Robinson, VC, accompanied by a friend, waved as the car slowly passed en route to the bustle of the railway station and the Station Master, resplendent in his uniform.

On Saturday, 16 September, Lt Robinson, VC, prepared for a night patrol. The wind had whipped up from the south-west in strong gusts. The flares burned brightly, illuminating the flight path, and the pungent smell of burnt, cotton waste soaked in paraffin wafted across the darkened field. The mechanics wheeled the aircraft into position and Billy climbed into the cockpit of the BE2C, warmed up the engine and, settling into his seat, taxied onto the flare-path. Opening up the engine, the aircraft swiftly rose into the air, when a sudden gust of wind swung it off course and the landing wheels caught a hedge; Robinson fought to right the crashing machine.

Within seconds the engine burst into flames. He hurriedly scrambled out of the cockpit and ran from the wreckage, unable to believe the turn of events. Sadly, he turned around to see the burning shell of his aircraft No 2693 in which he had only two weeks earlier fought the Schutte-Lanz SL11 to its destruction. The authorities were not amused at the potential risks taken by the new national hero and were alarmed at the news of the crash and Billy's lucky escape. Orders were issued for him to attend a series of official engagements and, while the high command were deciding his fate, he settled in to a round of social visits, at which his charm, good looks and sense of humour, made him an instant success.

The raids continued over England and on the dark and ominously quiet night of the 23/24 September 1916, the searchlights played nervously with the clouds. Shortly before 11.00pm the throb of heavy German engines was heard over Hornchurch and, within minutes, six bombs hurtled down towards the airfield, the huge explosions throwing mounds of earth skywards. Four bombs fell to the east of Suttons Farm, one by the old farmhouse. Another caused a large crater in the airfield, and the sixth fell to the west of the field. One Royal Flying Corps mechanic was injured but, luckily, relatively little damage was caused. The Zeppelin L32 droned on towards London, where it caused great damage to property and many persons were killed and injured during fierce opposition from Dartford's anti-aircraft defences.

Billy Robinson was on duty at the airfield, but Fred Sowrey was aloft, scouring the skies for the Hun. At 1.00am one of three ships, the L32, was intercepted by him and shot down at Billericay in Essex, where it burned for an hour, killing all the crew. Victoriously, Freddy returned to Suttons Farm to make out his report, jubilant at his success. Shortly afterwards, Billy at the wheel of a staff car, hurtled along the lanes towards the stricken airship, heavily loaded with Lt Sowrey, Capt Stammers, Lt C C Durston, and followed noisily by Lts Mallinson and Brock on their motorcycles. Unknown to them, Lt A de Bath Brandon had also brought down the Zeppelin L33 intact! The airship had come in from the north-east and dropped bombs on Bow and Bromley-by-Bow, damaging many houses, factories and commercial premises. It killed 11 persons and injured 25 residents. After jettisoning some of its gear to lighten the load, and being badly hit by anti-aircraft shells, it rose rapidly, making off towards the north-east. As the ship passed over Chelmsford in Essex, Lt de Bath Brandon engaged it, pursuing it to the coast where, losing gas badly and descending rapidly, it flew two miles out into the blackness of the North Sea. The Commander, realising his predicament, decided to return to the English coast, where the great vessel came down, low over the water, touching down just inland. The German crew set fire to the Zeppelin, then formed up and marched down the road to Colchester,

Essex, where they were met by a very surprised Special Constable and surrendered to him without trouble.

The loss of two of Germany's best airships was a blow to the enemy who had earlier reported in the Munich newspaper *Neueste Nachrichten*:

The glorious German aerial engines of war penetrate to England's heart, and London trembles before their attacks which it is hoped will be more frequent in future.

On 1 October 1916, the Evening Service had commenced at the Parish Church, Hornchurch, but before they were able to settle to the ceremony, the Special Constables were called from their pews as a Zeppelin raid had been reported. They left quietly to attend to their duties.

Eleven Zeppelins had left their sheds in Germany, ten of the ships crossing the coast. Three were Super Zeppelins, including the L31 commanded by Hauptmann Mathy. Crossing the coast at Lowestoft he passed over Chelmsford at 8.00pm, attempting to reach the capital, but came under intense anti-aircraft fire. He abandoned his attempt and dropped his bombs on Cheshunt, where they damaged 300 houses. Lt W J Tempest, a great friend of Billy Robinson, caught the Zeppelin on its escape route, firing drum after drum into the huge frameworek until it caught fire. The ship capsized with its nose alight, sloped downwards, and suddenly righted itself before it broke into two flaming sections, crashing at Potters Bar, where Mathy and all his crew perished in the flames. The personnel of Suttons Farm aerodrome were ecstatic at the successes and nobody slept that night. All four airmen, close friends, had victoriously drowned a 'Zepp' – the morale at the Station rose to unprecedented heights!

Gravestone at German War Graves Commission, Cannock Chase, Staffs, 1988   Photograph by Leslie Bills

11 Brief Encounter

The previous week's events began to tell on Billy; with lack of sleep and the strain of continuous night-flying, he needed a rest, as did his colleagues. Although Billy still awaited delivery of his new automobile, he and Freddy decided they would visit the town of Ilford at the next opportunity. A few days later they were in nearby Ilford, ready to relax for a while and enjoy the delights of that bustling town, and to spend some of his well-earned prize money.

They walked down from the railway station, passed the Hippodrome Theatre and the Black Horse Public House, and crossed the cobbled street, avoiding a noisy tram which rattled over the criss-crossed, metallic rails. They stood for a moment at the Clock Tower, watching the townsfolk busily going about their business and decided to walk to John Bodgers, Gentlemen's Outfitters, to savour the atmosphere of the store and buy some civilian clothes, which Billy hoped would help to avoid recognition wherever he appeared.

Freddy grinned as Billy flicked his 'lucky', bent halfpenny off his thumbnail – a souvenir of an encounter with a piece of shrapnel over Lille in May 1915.

'You'll lose that damned thing if you're not careful,' he laughed.

The coin spun into the air for the third time just as Freddy involuntarily jolted Billy's elbow.

'Look at those two over there!' he whispered.

Billy turned, the coin missed his hand and rolled across the pavement towards the high-buttoned boots which peeked tantalisingly from under a long, velvet skirt. Billy's trained eye quickly followed the coin as it came to rest at her feet. He raised his eyes to meet those of a pretty, young lady, who was grinning broadly, her eyes twinkling with mischief.

'Why, sir! you nearly lost it down the grating,' she said.

'Oh! come on Rosie,' her girlfriend said impatiently.

'No – please,' pleaded Billy, involuntarily panicking at the thought of losing such a delightful young flapper. 'Thank you, the coin is a talisman – I'd be lost without it,' he said hurriedly.

Freddy grinned, embarrassed at the encounter, nervously fingering his tie.

Rose Jones, 1917, then aged 17, died 1986. Author's mother
Author's collection

Tram Terminus and the Chequers Public House, Barkingside, Essex, c1905 *London Borough of Redbridge*

Billy, who had no intention of letting this lovely young thing go, rushed in with . . . 'It's a beautiful day and we have a few hours' leave before we fly again. Would you young ladies give us the pleasure of your company on a joy-ride?'

'We'd be honoured to travel with you sir, wouldn't we Florrie?' Rose replied.

'Well – er – yes – I suppose so,' her companion agreed.

They boarded an open-topped tram, laden with bags of fruit, which Billy had co-opted Freddy into buying from Prentis, the High Class Fruiterers in the High Road. Noisily clattering up the winding staircase, they settled onto the wooden-slatted seats at the front of the upper-deck of the tram – happily aloft to look down on the crowded streets below them.

'Four to Barkingside, return, please,' ordered Robinson.

'No charge to you and your companions, sir,' the conductress said gratuitously. 'Ain't you the bloke wot brought the Zepp down?'

William smiled and said nothing. Rose looked up at him, her eyes wide with admiration.

'Well, we both bagged one actually!' said Freddy proudly.

They giggled and laughed on the bumpy journey all the way to the tram terminous at Barkingside, resisted the temptation to call in at The Chequers for a 'London & Burton', and devoured large quantities of fruit instead. Robinson was most taken with Rosie, an Ilford girl, almost 17 years old, and quite beautiful. Her bubbly personality had relieved a great deal of the tension of the last few months. She was fun, with a delicious and warm sense of humour, matching his own. The two aviators escorted the girls to St Clements Road and left them at the gates of their respective residences, but not before Billy had arranged to meet Rose Jones later in the month.

73

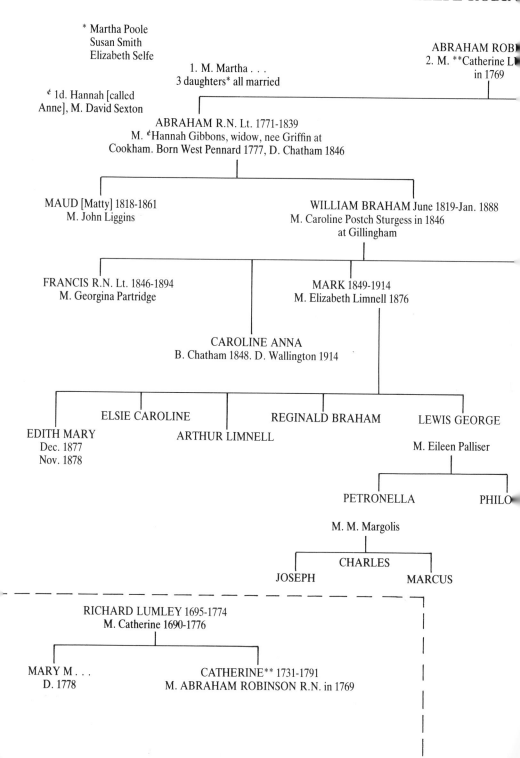

* Martha Poole
Susan Smith
Elizabeth Selfe

ABRAHAM ROB
2. M. **Catherine L
in 1769

1. M. Martha . . .
3 daughters* all married

ᵉ 1d. Hannah [called
Anne], M. David Sexton

ABRAHAM R.N. Lt. 1771-1839
M. ᵉHannah Gibbons, widow, nee Griffin at
Cookham. Born West Pennard 1777, D. Chatham 1846

MAUD [Matty] 1818-1861
M. John Liggins

WILLIAM BRAHAM June 1819-Jan. 1888
M. Caroline Postch Sturgess in 1846
at Gillingham

FRANCIS R.N. Lt. 1846-1894
M. Georgina Partridge

MARK 1849-1914
M. Elizabeth Limnell 1876

CAROLINE ANNA
B. Chatham 1848. D. Wallington 1914

ELSIE CAROLINE

REGINALD BRAHAM

LEWIS GEORGE

EDITH MARY
Dec. 1877
Nov. 1878

ARTHUR LIMNELL

M. Eileen Palliser

PETRONELLA

PHILO

M. M. Margolis

CHARLES

JOSEPH

MARCUS

RICHARD LUMLEY 1695-1774
M. Catherine 1690-1776

MARY M . . .
D. 1778

CATHERINE** 1731-1791
M. ABRAHAM ROBINSON R.N. in 1769

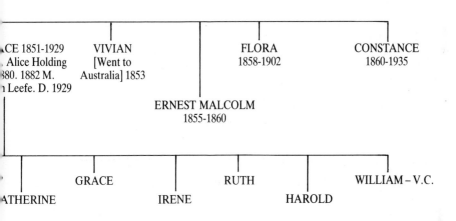

WILLIAM HENRY 1775-1841
M. Sarah Lee. Both buried in vault at
Cookham. 5 sons, 2 died young. 3 daughters, 1 married

CE 1851-1929
Alice Holding
880. 1882 M.
Leefe. D. 1929

VIVIAN
[Went to
Australia] 1853

ERNEST MALCOLM
1855-1860

FLORA
1858-1902

CONSTANCE
1860-1935

GRACE

ATHERINE

IRENE

RUTH

HAROLD

WILLIAM – V.C.

Clock Tower, Ilford Broadway, Essex. Built 1901, removed to South
Park 1923. Tower destroyed by enemy action 1944
London Borough of Redbridge

12 Tryst with a Hero

On 18 October 1916, Lt William Leefe Robinson, VC, was informed of his promotion to Flight Commander, with a confirmation of temporary, acting Captain, and an increase of pay backdated to 1 September. He was still not flying, and asked to be sent to France, but instead was advised of a posting to the command of the Home Defence Squadrons in Northern England and Scotland. He was unhappy at the thought of being transferred to a northern airfield, and was disappointed at his failure to continue flying, but there was always the quiet interlude with feminine company to help forget the traumas and stress of service life.

He longed to visit his mother in India and, in his quiet moments, wondered what was happening in Co-org.

During one such period of isolation, he travelled in his 'Prince Henry' through the country lanes towards Ilford, the autumn hues of colour falling from the English oaks and elms, forming a carpet of leaves en route to the bustle of the town, and an engagement with a delightful, young lady – Rose Jones.

Billy turned into Clements Road and stopped the 25hp Vauxhall Prince Henry (so called for its success in the German Prince Henry trials of 1910/11) outside the Post Office opposite the residence of the local builder, William Henry Jones. Numerous telegraph boys immediately congregated around the machine as the Royal Flying Corps officer hurried across the road to knock on the door of No 10. Many curtains fluttered at the neighbours' windows as Rose swept across the street on the arm of the handsome aviator, her broad-brimmed, flower-trimmed hat firmly held to her head, as the gusty wind flipped up her fox fur. He opened the door for her, then hurried around the car, swinging a booted leg over the spare wheel to leap smartly into the driver's seat.

'Princess for a day, dear girl,' he said. 'Let's go to the castle at Cranbrook.' She smiled happily. 'What a lovely idea, Billy.' She could not believe this was happening and tried hard not to wave to a number of her acquaintances as they sped along the Cranbrook Road.

'Was your friend annoyed that I did not invite her out as well?' he asked.

'No, she was glad really – she's married you see.'

Cranbrook Castle, *c*1900 (built 1765, demolished in 1923)
London Borough of Redbridge

Miss Rose Jones   *Author's collection*

Ilford Broadway, Essex, *c*1907   *London Borough of Redbridge*

High Road, Ilford, Essex, *c*1912 showing Clements Road (near tram) and the Cinema De Luxe (No. 98). Nearby Gerrards Ltd Restaurant (No. 104)   *London Borough of Redbridge*

'I'm pleased you were able to come,' he laughed. 'I'm fed up with people, it's no joke, old girl, being feted wherever you go – it's nice to be alone – well, alone with you that is – to talk of things other than Zeppelins!' he said with feeling.

'Where do you come from, not Scotland?' she enquired.

'Good Lord! No, I was born in India. It is very beautiful there, you would love it,' he enthused.

'My half-brother, Bill, died in India, he was a soldier, so it has unhappy memories for me,' replied Rose, her doe-like eyes looking up at him.

The car swung off the road onto the grassland where Billy stopped at the low-gated entrance to the castle. They wandered round the castle with its castellated, brick towers looming formidably above them, its quaint-shaped windows, neither Gothic nor Rectangular.

'Strange looking place,' Billy reflected.

'I think it's a folly – a gentleman's fancy,' Rose said wisely.

He laughed. 'Like you Rosie?' he invited.

She turned and looked straight into his twinkling blue eyes. 'I'm not one of your Zepps you know – an easy target!'

'My darling girl,' he whispered, slipping his arm around her shoulders, 'I'm not only an officer, but a gentleman and, to prove it, let us find a restaurant, and eat and be merry!' He smiled, and the corners of his moustache lifted invitingly. She turned and looked at him, knowing she was powerless to resist this man who had recently killed 16 Germans.

They returned down Cranbrook Road, passed the Hippodrome Theatre, opposite the Clock Tower, and stopped at 'Jerrards', an exclusive restaurant in the High Road. They hurried passed the fairytale window of Alf Wood, the Jeweller, through the doors of the restaurant, held open by the proprietor who welcomed them warmly and led them to a dimly lit table.

'I haven't been in here before – it is lovely!' Rose said.

'Nor I,' Billy answered quietly, leaning across the table. 'It is an affluent little town, Ilford – at least on the outside.'

'My father calls it "Pride and Poverty",' laughed Rose.

'What on earth for?' exclaimed Billy.

'Well! he says he's seen sisters wear each other's clothes – he believes they wear them each in turn,' Rose giggled.

Billy laughed. 'I shall take special notice of sisters in future . . . I have four sisters – haven't seen them for an age,' he said thoughtfully.

They sat silently, just the clicking of knife and fork. Rose was conscious of the eyes of other customers looking at them. She realised what a well-known officer she was with and, in a moment of panic in cutting through the portion of succulent meat, the knife slipped and shot numerous green peas across the floor of the restaurant. Rose was horrified and wished the

80

floor would open up and devour her embarrassment! Heads turned, noses went up, then returned to the meal in hand. Billy quickly clicked his fingers and beckoned the waiter over, who hurried to the table.

'More peas for madam,' he ordered. 'Don't worry, Rosie,' he smiled, touching her hand.

'What do you think of when you are flying – it must be cold up there?' Rose broke the silence.

'Flying is the most beautiful experience – alone in an aircraft at 8,000ft. Yes, it is cold, but the clouds are many different colours and the view of the ground is unbelievable. It is difficult to describe, but I love flying – you are like a bird – no restrictions, at peace with your maker. To see the smoke trailing behind a train, the glittering ribbon of light that is a river – you would be enthralled, Rosie.'

'I'd be terrified!' exclaimed Rose.

They sat silently in the dim light – Rose wide-eyed and beautiful – Billy Robinson, valiant hero of the air, handsome and appealing – their eyes devouring each other.

'Will I see you again?' Rose appealed.

'I have asked to go to France,' he replied. 'I don't know, perhaps we shall, I hope so.'

He left her by the gate of No 10 – she waved and turned hurriedly away.

He travelled silently back to Suttons Farm airfield – not singing as he usually did.

She sobbed quietly until the early hours of the morning.

Victoria Cross awarded to Lt W.L. Robinson 'For Valour'
Christie's

13 The Waiting Game

Robinson settled to the routine of the Home Defence Squadron at Suttons Farm, reflecting on the 2,000-3,000 individual subscriptions he had received which ranged from one penny to 2s. 6d (12½p). Pressure to appear at public functions mounted daily. The Parish Council of Hornchurch decided to present a silver cup to Lt Leefe Robinson, VC, and wrote inviting him to a presentation at the New Zealand Camp at Grey Towers Park, but Billy, in typical sportsmanlike fashion, replied suggesting the gift be shared with his friend, Freddy Sowrey, who likewise had brought down a 'Zepp'. The Committee impressed by his generous suggestion, agreed to purchase two cups but, whilst these were being inscribed, Lt Tempest had successfully shot down a third airship, and they decided to present a third silver cup. On 14 October 1916, the very handsome cups were presented to Robinson and Sowrey at an occasion presided over by Mr Thomas Gardner, JP, CC, the presentation being made by Mr W H Legg, the Chairman of Hornchurch Parish Council. The cup was inscribed:

Presented by the residents of Hornchurch, Essex, as as token of admiration and gratitude to Lieutenant William Leefe Robinson, VC, Worcestershire Regiment and Royal Flying Corps. Lieutenant Robinson with conspicuous bravery attacked and destroyed an enemy aeroplane under circumstances of great difficulty and danger during the night of September 2/3rd 1916.

A similar cup was presented to Lt F Sowrey, DSO, but, due to duties elsewhere, Lt Tempest was unable to be present at the gathering of the large and enthusiastic audience.

One of Billy's admirers at this time was Mrs Joan Whipple, who frequently visited Suttons Farm aerodrome with friends from her days at Bentley Priory, Stanmore. Joan was the widow of Capt Herbert Connell Whipple, of the Devonshire Regiment, who had been killed in action in December 1914. Billy was very impressed with her and, despite strong competition for his favours, he announced their engagement to be married.

Later in September the Germans lost another four airships as a result of a bombing raid on London, which had wrought havoc in Piccadilly Circus, killing and injuring many people, as well as the destruction of buildings. The raid was surrounded in mystery, with stories of the massive Zeppelins drifting helplessly at various places on the Continent.

In October 1916 Robinson wrote to his mother:

Dear old 'G' who will be with you when you receive this will tell you something of the letters and telegrams I have received. The day after I was awarded the VC I received 37 telegrams, which includes one from my colonel and one from General Henderson, who is of course the boss of the whole RFC.

I have had tons of interviews too, amongst which are those I have had with – The Grand Duke Michle(??!) of Russia, Lord Curzon, General Sir David Henderson and heaps of others. When I went to Windsor to get the VC The King was awfully nice, asking me all about you dear people and Grandfather etc, and showed me some awfully interesting photographs taken from the air over the German Lines.

G will tell you all about the 4 days leave I had at Southbourne with her.

Oh, I could go on telling you what I have done and go on writing for a month of Sundays, but I must cut things short. I have, of course had hundreds of invitations most of which I have had to refuse owing to duty.

I went up to Newcastle for a day and was entertained by the Lord Mayor who gave a dinner in my honour, where I was presented with a cheque for £2,000 by Col Cowen of Newcastle. They wanted to make the whole thing a grand public function but HQ wouldn't let them, for which I was very thankful.

I've had endless other small presents – some of the nicest are the paintings of the burning Zepp.

By the by about 5 artists have offered to paint my portrait for the RA.

As I daresay you have seen in the papers – Babies, flowers and hats have been named after me also poems and prose have been dedicated to me – oh, its too much!

I am recognised wherever I go about Town now, whether in uniform or mufti – The city police salute me – The waiters, Hall porters and pages of Hotels and Restaurants bow and scrape – visitors turn round and stare – Oh its too thick!

But the most glorious thing is that Sowrey, dear old boy, and Tempest, sweet soul, the two Zepp strafers who have been awarded DSOs are both in my flight!! Some flight – five officers, of which there are two DSOs and a VC and three Zepps to our credit – some record!!!

Well you darlings I'll close now or else I'll go babbling on all night and I'm really tired.

I'll just tell you I'm not at present at Hornchurch, I'm somewhere in England on a secret mission but I'm going back to dear old Sutton's Farm again.

Well, do forgive me for not writing before.

Ever Your loving son
Billy

The months went slowly for Billy Robinson after the excitement of his victory. With no flying duties and only regular public relation appearances, as a morale booster for the citizens of the country, he once again volunteered for duties in France. It was on 9 February 1917 that a

William's mother Elizabeth (known as Bessie) in later years (died
1929)   *Mrs R. David*

posting came through for 48 Squadron located at Rendcombe, Gloucestershire, and with great relief Billy Robinson reported to Major L. Parker as a Flight Commander. Equipped with the new Bristol F2a fighter, eighteen biplanes flew to Bertangles in France on 18 March 1917. The 'Brisfit', as it was known to the pilots, was a great improvement on the old BE2cs Robinson had flown in the past. It was a two-seater fighter, armed with a synchronized Vickers machine gun for the pilot and a Lewis gun for the observer, and was a robust and manoeuvrable aircraft with a speed of 123mph. Its debut on the Western Front was to be disastrous for the Royal Flying Corps and for Billy Robinson.

14 Return to France

On Christmas Day 1915, a young 23-year-old German passed his third and final examination to become a pilot. The son of a soldier in the 1st Regiment of Cuirassiers in Breslau, Manfred von Richthofen, a country boy, was educated privately until he was 10 years old. A year later he became a cadet in Wahlstaff and prepared for a military career, being accepted into the 1st Regiment of Uhlans. He had not liked the strict discipline of the training, nor was he inclined to an academic career, excelling at gymnastics and football. He loved riding and his ability as a horseman gave him the trained eye and quick reflexes necessary for a fighter pilot. He spent the earlier part of the First World War in a cavalry unit, fighting the French Cuirassiers at the Battle of Virton and later at Verdun, where he soon became bored with inactivity as a despatch bearer. On off-duty nights he would enjoy his favourite pastime of game shooting and, in the forest of La Chausée, on beautiful moonlit nights, would hunt wild pigs. On one such expedition he stalked and finally shot a pig he affectionately called 'Auntie Pig' as she swam across a river at midnight. His restless attitude to his superiors finally secured a transfer to the German Flying Service.

At seven o'clock on the morning of 26 December 1915, with mounting excitement, he flew for the first time as an observer. On climbing into the machine he found he was unable to communicate with the pilot due to the noise of the engine. He tried to pass messages by paper, but these disappeared in the draught from the propeller, and he felt most uncomfortable, losing helmet and scarf in the slipstream! Clutching the sides of the cockpit coaming he peered over the side, enthralled by the pretty view of the ground from the air, with the tiny, toy-like Cathedral of Cologne in the distance. He enjoyed it so much that he found his impatience rising as the long hours passed until the next airborne adventure, apprehensive lest the war should end without a chance to go to the front line. By June 1915 he was sent to the Russian front and carried out reconnaissance patrols twice a day, bringing back valuable information on the battles between Gorlice and Brest-Litovsk.

Over the countryside, burning with the carnage of war, he was shot down in company with an expert pilot named Count Holck. The

'Albatross' two-seater landed near a wood, complete with the Count's pet dog, who would normally lie on a fur rug in the cockpit. Fortunately, the German advance had prevented them from falling into the hands of the Russians, who would have killed them, as they did not take kindly to aviators who shot at them from the skies. Prussian Guardsmen gave them two horses to return to the airfield – unfortunately for the Count, the dog was not seen again.

In the latter part of 1915 Von Richthofen was to meet a German fighter pilot, Oswald Boelcke, who at that time had shot down four enemy machines and gained valuable knowledge of tactics. Intensive training and a battered aircraft caused by a bad landing encouraged the young pilot to finalise his examinations in Berlin. On 26 April 1916, in an Albatross flying machine, he shot down a Nieuport Scout flown by a novice pilot at Fleury, south and west of Douaumont. Hauptmann Boelcke pioneered many of the tactics used in air combat and Von Richthofen was greatly influenced by his techniques. Boelcke was killed on 28 October 1916, in a collision with a fellow pilot's machine flown by Lt Erwin Boehme. He was credited with 40 victories. He taught the advantages gained by superior height over your enemy, better speed and that of cover, preferably with the sun behind the attacking aircraft. He would approach the blind spot on the tail of the victim and close to within 50yds before attacking. Manfred von Richthofen quickly learned the strength of a team spirit to enable fellow pilots to watch the skies to ensure the attacking pilot was not pounced upon whilst setting up his own machine for an attack. Another German pilot, Max Immelmann, had earlier perfected a manoeuvre to pull his aircraft up as if to loop, half roll the machine at the top of the loop and come out in the opposite direction, thereby gaining altitude while turning. This surprise tactic took many allied pilots by surprise – to their cost! During late 1915 and early 1916 the Fokker EIII, single-seater, fighter began to worry the British. It was fast and very manoeuvrable. To regain the initiative, the French re-equipped their *escadrilles de chasse* with Nieuport Scouts in larger numbers and air superiority was regained over Verdun. The offensive tactics of Maj-Gen H.M. Trenchard, Commander of the Royal Flying Corps, were to supply aircraft of one type to the squadrons in their specialist roles, doing away with many of the machines that were both old and unsuitable for the various task allotted to each unit. Wings were combined into brigades; of the two wings in each brigade, one, the Corps Wing, carried out artillery observations, close reconnaissance photography and bombing, working for the Corps Headquarters; whilst the Army Wing, responsible to an Army Headquarters, mounted offensive patrols, long-range reconnaissance and bombing flights, fought the enemy in the air, and protected the Corps aircraft.

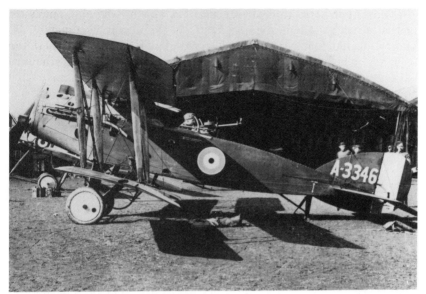

Bristol Fighter F2A, cApril 1917. Robinson shot down in No.
A3337   *Imperial War Museum*

Pilots of Jasta II, 23 April 1917. Vizefeldwebel Sebastian Festner,
third from left standing – Richthofen in cockpit   *Imperial War
Museum*

The German reply to the reorganisation was to form units solely of fighter aircraft called the Jagdstaffeln (Hunting Section). Each Jagdstaffeln had fourteen machines, some with the new Halberstadt DII, a single-seater biplane to replace the obsolete Fokkers but, as its speed was only 90mph it was quickly replaced by the Albatross DII and DIII. Boelcke commanded Jagdstaffel (Jasta) 2, and one of his pilots was Manfred von Richthofen. The success of the unit was confirmed when they destroyed four British machines without loss to themselves during September 1916. By the spring of 1917 thirty-seven Jastas were operating along the battlefront. Upon the death of Boelcke, Manfred von Richthofen quickly took over the leadership of the Jasta 2. Manfred, disciplined and ambitious, thrived on his new command. His pilots, all hand picked, were both skilled and fearless. In early March 1917, von Richthofen had a personal 'score' of thirty victories and his all-red Albatross DIII, in tight formation with the rest of his colourful 'circus' of machines, was a formidable sight to the allies.

British pilots were being sent to France with less than 20hrs' solo flying to their credit and only a few hours' experience of the type of aircraft they were allocated to fly! With many inexperienced pilots flying unfamiliar machines over an area to which they were unaccustomed, the predictable result was called 'Bloody April' by the Royal Flying Corps. The life expectancy of a pilot arriving at the front varied between eleven days and three weeks. During this time, of the 360 RFC aircraft in use on the Western Front, 150 were lost in April, with 316 pilots and observers either killed or missing.

Into this battle Billy Robinson took off from La Bellevue airfield on 5 April 1917, leading a flight of six new Bristol F2a, two-seater fighters. Billy led the patrol in a tight formation in the belief that more protection was given to individual members of the flight. The potential of the new aircraft was not realised at the earlier stages of its use and, with his observer, Lt Edward Warburton, he considered that, with untried crews, a defensive position would be the safest.

Rittmeister Manfred Freiherr von Richthofen, leading a kette of Albatross DIII fighters from Jagdstaffel II, approached the 'foreign gentlemen' over Arras with his usual aggressive spirit, borne of confidence and determination, to tackle the English pilots, whom he believed were both daring and stupid. He conceded that, in the eyes of the British pilots, they probably considered they were both plucky and brave in a fight. He mused on, mentally respecting the sporting instincts of his foes. The five, twin machine gun fighters rapidly closed with the flight of 'Brisfits' in a manoeuvre resembling a cavalry charge! The British fighters broke formation and scattered under the hail of fire as the 'packing cases' (as the Germans referred to their machines) roared into their midst, a circus of colour, spitting death. A number of English guns refused to work, as the lubricating oil had frozen in the mechanism. Vizefeldwebel Sebastian Festner did not realise his opponent was a 'Zepp' killer – fortunately for Robinson! The bullets ripped into the engine of Robinson's aircraft and the machine shuddered under the impact. Using all his skill, Billy brought the machine down in a field near Mericourt, behind the German lines. They clambered out and Billy grabbed the Lewis gun and fired at the inquisitive Festner as he circled victoriously over the damaged aircraft, before he flew off to secure a further kill and return to his airfield.

Richthofen's pilots were very pleased with the events of the day, having shot down thirteen aircraft with a loss of only six machines. Four of Robinson's flight had been brought down – a disastrous day for No 48 Squadron.

Robinson and Warburton were immediately captured. They were held for a few days in Karlsruhe, near Stuttgart, and then transferred to a prisoner-of-war camp in Freiburg-im-Breisgsau, south-west of Karlsruhe, near the Swiss border.

The next day, Richtofen's Jasta 2 brought down a further eight allied aircraft, including five Nieuport Scouts. Eighteen days later Festner was shot down and died of his wounds.

The 'Brisfit' redeemed its capabilities, as experience built up amongst the crews. With synchronized Vickers machine guns for the pilots and a Lewis gun for the observers, they were robust and manoeuvrable aircraft. The increased speed of 123mph made it an effective weapon. Whilst flying these Bristol fighters, No 48 Squadron destroyed 148 enemy aircraft.

Rittmeister Manfred von Richthofen (eighty victories)   *Imperial War Museum*

15 Prisoner of War

Robinson and Warburton were despatched quickly to Karlsruhe for a few days before they were taken the sixty miles to the prisoner-of-war camp at Freiburg-im-Breisgau, their first experience of a secure confinement in the enemy hands. The news of the event soon circulated to the stunned nation in England and many feared Robinson had been killed, not the least his fiancée, who was distraught at the news from the battlefront. The anxious moments were soon dispelled when letters reached Joan Whipple and his parents, in which he confirmed his well-being, bemoaning capture, but with his sense of humour always belittling the facts. The Germans were well aware of the fame of their prisoner, and from very recent experience of adulation in England, he found for the first time personal hatred from the camp guards. Robinson's letters home gave no hint of the maltreatment of prisoners, nor of his own problems which frequently made life very unpleasant.

With certain lines censored by his captors, he wrote to his parents:

I have written two sheets to the best girl on God's earth – Joan, and have reserved this one sheet for you dear old people. I believe I have already written one letter or PC to you from this place Freiburg, at any rate if I haven't Joan will tell you all about it, and how I was transferred to this camp here from Karlsruhe with 19 other officers at the beginning of last month . . . [Three lines censored]. We are really very comfortable here and altogether a very lazy crew. I have two other officers in my room both of whom are receiving parcels so we feed awfully well, and start off with a regular English Breakfast of porridge and bacon every morning – and sausages when we have them. I've got things going here a bit by now. We've formed a committee and I've started a library of English books (Taychnetz edition) we've already got just over 100 books. We are also getting up a sports club, and hope to get a club room out of the German authorities which we'll fit up as comfortably as we can. So you see life is quite pleasant here – although of course one gets awfully sick sometimes when you think that if things had been a little different we would still be on the same side of the wire doing something instead of slacking here out of it all as it were!

Many of the inmates of the prison camp considered it a duty to try to escape and return to active service and Robinson's thoughts constantly turned to the best method of escape from his captors and, although others had elected to sit out the war, the majority, like Billy, tried every opportunity to depart from Freiburg. With three other officers, Billy's earlier attempts to tunnel under the walls of the building came to nothing, and their thoughts turned to more subtle ways of escaping.

On 21 July 1917 Robinson again wrote to his parents:

In a letter I received from dear little Joan yesterday I learnt of the sad news of Grace's death. I can't tell you what a terrible shock it was – we understood one another so well – I might have done so much more for her. I might have been a far more dutiful brother. And what gives me such pain is thinking you dear ones will have to bear this so many miles away from most of your children. How I wish I were with you so that I could try and bring you some comfort in my own poor way. But as I said to Joan, such a loss as this makes me prize more, if possible those who are still left to me – Joan comes first in one way, you two darlings come first in another. I firmly believe that sorrow does not come into our lives, and go without leaving some good behind – this extra bond of love and sympathy may not be the only good this intense sorrow has left.

After Arthur's death I believe the dear girl was never quite happy – but pray God she has perfect happiness now, and for that let us all be glad to sacrifice our own feelings. There is a Divine purpose in all things. How I love you dear ones at home – Mother darling you still have your baby boy – for I am always that – and he will always love you dearly and do anything in this world for you.

I am wonderfully well here at present and we have a very good time on the whole. We have founded a debating society now, and have arranged for debates to be held every Tuesday evening. We went to the swimming baths as usual yesterday morning and for a glorious walk afterwards. After climbing a hill we had a lovely view of Freiburg and the surrounding country – which is very beautiful about these parts. I must close now darlings – you know you have the deepest sympathy from your loving son.

In collusion with 2/Lt Baerlin of No 16 Squadron, they tried to bribe a guard, who readily accepted the money, but attempts to get away were frustrated by the Camp Commandant, and they were promptly arrested and formally charged. Not to be daunted, Billy Robinson tried to escape again on 18 September 1917, before the Court Martial was held. Fellow prisoners hung clothes on a washing line to conceal the small party of escapees, unlocked the door of a courtyard and awaited events. Robinson's orderly, an ex-locksmith, refused at the last minute to pick the lock of the last gate before freedom for fear of being caught, and would not make the short journey across the cobbled yard – the attempt failed and their captors were unaware of the planned escape. Within hours a fourth attempt was planned, the conspirators deciding on another tunnel escape. An old timber shed provided cover for the digging operation and this revealed a staircase leading into an adjoining church. Exhausted from digging, they finally gathered in the aisle, forced open a window and silently dropped into the deserted, but familiar street below. The party split up and Robinson and Baerlin, together with another fellow officer, hurriedly made their way out of town in the direction of the Swiss border, some thirty-five miles to the south. Four days later, within a few miles of Stuhlingen, they were recaptured by an alert sentry and returned, unceremoniously, to the prison camp, tired and dispirited. The authorities were not amused by the determination of their foes and Robinson was court martialled and sentenced to one month's solitary confinement in Zorndorf prison camp.

Zorndorf was a bleak and formidable prison, with little chance of escape. The dark and dank cells were approached by long underground tunnels. The single exit was up a long, sloping tunnel which emerged in the centre of a mound of earth ringed by barbed wire, and illuminated by searchlights. Billy suffered from claustrophobia and solitary confinement in the twilight of the prison cell was a traumatic experience for him, that was neither enlightened by the harsh treatment by the guards, nor the food from the squalid cookhouse.

On 18 May 1918, he was transferred with two other officers to Clausthal prison camp in the Harz mountains. The train journey was an opportunity not to be missed by the trio and they decided one of them must stay to distract the guards whilst the other two escaped through the carriage door. Robinson was furthest from the door and the guards overpowered him before he could jump to freedom.

At Clausthal, Billy Robinson came face to face with Heinrich Niemeyer, Camp Commandant, twin brother of the infamous Karl Niemeyer of Holzminden prison camp. The brothers were feared by both friend and foe and rivalled each other in arrogance and deceit. They both had 'bullet heads', with close-cropped hair, florid complexions, grey moustachios, curled as the Kaiser, heavy jowls and thick necks. Smartly dressed in Prussian, military great-coats, and with 'spurs' on their boots, they presented an unrelenting tower of complete authority over other men. They had both lived in the province of Milwaukee, USA, for 17 years and spoke English, underlined with American slang. Heinrich was extremely vile and objectionable and took an immediate dislike to Billy Robinson, whose reputation had preceded him. The camp was an improvement on his month in Clausthal and he was not denied the normal privileges afforded officers. He was amused to be given a 'pass card' allowing him occasional visits outside the camp, which read:

By this card I give my word of honour that during the walks outside the camp I will not escape nor attempt to make an escape nor will I attempt to commit any action during this time to the prejudice of the German Empire. I hereby give my word of honour to use this card only myself and not give it to any other prisoner of war.

Capt William Leefe Robinson, VC, was 23 years of age on 14 July 1918, and shortly after his birthday was transferred to the notorious prison camp at Holzminden, into the 'care' of Hauptmann Karl Niemeyer, to be disciplined by a patriotic German who loved his fatherland and hated the

British. Billy heard that 'Charles' had been given a command on the Somme, but had shortly afterwards been relieved of that responsibility. The Commandant's facetious and offensive remarks were well-known, but his instant dislike of Robinson was to take the form of ceaseless and methodical persecution of the British airman, who was known to the Germans as the 'English Richthofen', who was also responsible for the destruction of the Schutte-Lanz SL11 which crashed in flames with the loss of many German airmen.

Billy took some comfort in reading and re-reading the many letters that he received through the Red Cross organisation, and one such letter from an admirer made him realise how the fortunes of war so rapidly change:

Dear Captain Robinson:

I have been knitting a woollen scarf, and I want you to have it, as you are the first VC airman of this war, in England. My mother wrote to Captain Sowrey to find out your address. I dare say you remember that about a year ago, mother sent you your photograph to autograph. We have it in our dining room, framed, with a Union Jack over it. I have got two photographs of you in my bedroom, and in every other room in the house there is one. I do hope you will get the parcel alright, as I do not want someone, whom I don't know, or of whom I have never heard, to have it, as I have taken a great deal of trouble over the scarf.

With kindest regards, I remain
Annie C Rogers

Robinson realised that to stay in the camp would ensure the personal attention of Karl Niemeyer, who had one objective in view – to break Robinson's spirit. Billy decided to attempt, yet again, to escape from Holzminden and return to his beloved Joan, marry her and return to India. He soon realised that a massive plan to escape by tunnelling out of the prison had been going on for many months previous to his transfer and immediately made known his interest in escaping. Dismayed at the sixty applicants already on the 'escape list', he waited patiently for the days to pass. On 24 July 1918 the Adjutant of the Camp, H G Durnford, checked his list of escapees, waiting until the German sentry had made his last inspection at 10.00pm. He visited all the rooms warning each man to get their kit ready and get into bed fully clothed to wait until called. Whispers went round of the escape and an air of excitement prevailed in the failing light. Carrying boots in hand and clad in stocking feet, they crept stealthily along the corridors. The working party for the final length of the 130yd tunnel had reached the field of rye outside the camp and had escaped by 1.15am. At 4.30am twenty-nine prisoners had gone through the tunnel, but then a Capt Gardiner reported that the tunnel was blocked by a prisoner getting stuck, with those following unable to proceed further. The Adjutant ordered an evacuation of the tunnel of heavy packs and men struggling and gasping for air, who could neither move forward or back.

Fortunately, a New Zealand officer called Garland, who was exceptionally strong, retrieved the rearmost man and baggage back to the entrance to the tunnel, dripping with sweat and exhausted. Four other men were still stuck in the tunnel at 5.30am. Part of the tunnel had collapsed, but the remaining four officers managed to get back to the building, covered in mud. Needless to say, Karl Niemeyer was not amused when he received the report of the escape of the prisoners and heard the laughter of the inmates as news spread quickly around the camp. From that time, open warfare existed between inmates and guards. Over the next two weeks a number of the officers were caught and returned to the camp, to be subjected to the fury of the Camp Commandant, who could not establish any tangible evidence of any conspiracy to damage German property and so bring serious charges. His frustration mounted as he inwardly seethed at not being able to find the ringleaders, and the day after the escape a sentry brutally kicked a Royal Flying Corps officer, and a further complaint was made by the Senior Officer to Niemeyer of injustice to various officers. This action was unusual, in alleging that conditions in the camp were monstrous and would not be acceptable according to the rules of the Hague Convention. A policy of passive resistance was agreed by the 500 officers in the camp.

It was in this atmosphere that Billy Robinson and a fellow officer, Capt W S Stephenson of 73 Squadron, escaped and were recaptured. The anger of Karl Niemeyer was intense. The Commandant considered it a personal attack on himself, aimed at damaging still further his position of authority and affronting his dignity. Robinson was, once again, thrown into solitary confinement. Niemeyer raged and fumed at Billy, shouting abuse in his American slang. 'You can't fool me, I know damn all see!' The Englishman was in serious trouble and at a great disadvantage to defend himself. The ground floor of the four-storey building, Kaserne 'A', of the Offizier Gefangenen (Officer Prisoner of War Camp) Lager, where Billy was confined, was a more secure prison than its nearby twin, architectural monstrosity, its lower windows never open. Billy began to lose heart in the stale, oppressive atmosphere of the sparsely furnished cell. Sleep was interrupted at regular intervals throughout the night by a Feldwebel, who would flash a torchlight into the faces of the occupants of the cells, causing them more distress, Billy received more attention from the guards and, in particular, Karl Niemeyer, who was determined to break his spirit.

A bout of the 'Spanish' influenza virus swept through the camp and resistance on the meagre diet became more difficult daily.

The word spread around the camp of the outrageous treatment meted out to the young man, and the incensed Senior British Officer arranged for a message to be smuggled out in the hollowed out handle of a tennis racquet which was transported in the care of an 'exchange' officer, lucky enough to be transferred back to England. The message was sent to the War Office in London, but Hauptmann Karl Niemeyer continued his sadistic, but subtle, treatment of the airman in retaliation for the killing of his friend, Willi Schramm. The guards nicknamed Billy 'Redfly' and, fearing reprisals from the Commandant, relentlessly carried out the harsh treatment demanded of them by their superior. The guards knew from bitter experience that discipline of his soldiers could be even more severe than that meted out to the British Officers.

Nevertheless, it is recorded that, the 'Chamber of Horrors', as the rooms devoted to 'special' prisoners were known, were, on occasions, the scene of humorous incidents, often caused by Lt Beyfus, who would ensure that the opening of his cell door coincided with him undressing, impinging onto some part of his anatomy, thus allowing him to curse the Germans who had made an attack on his person in a state of semi-nakedness wearing only his shirt!

The 'flu swept through the prison affecting both the Germans and the British until every room in the camp had some unfortunate victim groaning and hoping he was not about to die. Niemeyer succumbed to the virus, but quickly recovered, much to the disappointment of the British.

A visit by a representative of the German War Office, in reply to official complaints from the British High Command came to nothing, as Niemeyer, acting as interpreter, ensured that the facts were hidden, and convinced the inquirer that they had been exaggerated. The visiting German Officer went away satisfied there was nothing amiss at the camp, and found Niemeyer 'really quite a pleasant fellow'. Shortly after the ringleaders of the tunnel escape were transferred to another camp, including Captain H G Durnford, the Camp Adjutant, leaving Billy Robinson to 'rot' with Karl Niemeyer.

As the British advanced across the battlefields in their victorious battles of September 1918, Niemeyer softened in his attitude toward the prisoners, even to the extent of removing the Kaiser's picture from the wall of his office. By Armistice Day in November, Billy was a sick man and Karl Niemeyer had disappeared from the scene of his prison activities. Both brothers were on the 'black list' communicated by the Allied Supreme Council to the German Government.

The first tentative request for an armistice was made by the German Government to President Wilson of the United States of America on 5 October 1918. The Supreme War Council of the Allies sat in session at Versailles to decide the terms to be offered to enemy countries. Before dawn on 11 November 1918, the armistice was signed in Marshall Foch's special train in the forest of Compiègne, near Rethondes.

Captain William Leefe Robinson, VC was repatriated to England on 14 December 1918.

16 Return to Blighty

Christmas at Lavender Cottage, Gordon Avenue, Stanmore, the home of Capt Noel Clifton, was one of both rejoicing at Billy's return and sadness at his low state of health. With his fiancée, Joan Whipple, at his bedside, anxious moments were passed to ensure his happiness, knowing that the ordeal of the prison camp had extracted a great deal from the returned aviator. Baroness Heyking, his sister, had travelled from the South Coast to be with him, and no effort was spared to ensure his comfort, but a virulent influenza epidemic sweeping the country was too much for him to contend with and on 31 December 1918, Capt William Leefe Robinson, VC, died, aged 23 years, with his sister Kitty and his beloved Joan by his bedside.

He was as handsome in death as in life, and it was tragic to cover that brave heart, now still, which had fought so valiantly for England. It was difficult to accept the silence of the cottage without his courageous good humour and the warmth of the smile that had captivated the hearts of a grateful nation. Joan picked up the letter that had slipped to the floor, and she read:

Dear Robbie:

Won't it be lovely when the war's over? All our loved ones home again. Captain Sowrey wrote to us this week – he still adores and loves you. His letters are full of 'dear Robin' . . . The garden is looking lovely and the roses are perfect . . .

She placed the letter on the table, the paper moist with the frustration of a dream unfulfilled.

England mourned the passing of one of its most popular war heroes, and the funeral, which was held at Harrow Weald on Friday, 3 January 1919, was attended by many hundreds of people. The procession set out from Lavender Cottage, as a flight of aircraft, led by Brigadier T C Higgins, the Commander of the South East Home Defence Squadrons in 1916, flew overhead, and a large wreath was dropped before the house. Together with a large cross of flowers from his fiancée, Mrs Robinson's 'baby boy' was carried, with many other floral tributes on the coffin, to the tiny Harrow Weald Cemetery by All Saints Church. The Central Band of the Royal Air Force led the procession, the coffin borne on an Air Force trailer, in company with many officers from the Home Defence Squadrons and servicemen from Hounslow and Northolt through the lines of silent mourners. The muffled bells of All Saints rang out 720 Grandshire Doubles as Major Freddy Sowrey, DSO, and Major Noel Chiton led the pall bearers towards the graveside. Sgt Major Murrell, Chief Royal Air Force trumpeter, sounded the last post. As if to carry Billy Robinson once more into the heavens, his comrades placed a large, white floral tribute in the form of his coveted 'Wings' beside his resting place.

The *Daily Sketch* wrote:

As unassumingly as he bore his honours, as quietly as he had come from captivity to die, Captain Leefe Robinson, the 'Cuffley V.C.' – the first man to bring down a Zeppelin on English soil – was yesterday laid to rest in the cemetery of Harrow Weald. Only his relatives and a few intimate and chosen comrades of the air attended the hero's body to the grave, but the women and children to whom he brought a sense of safety made an informal guard of honour.

A stone border was placed around the grave. The epitaph read:

He was the first airman to attack an airship at night. After a most daring, single-handed flight he brought down L21 a flaming wreck on the 3rd September, 1916. Thus he led the way against the German Zeppelin peril threatening England.

The memorial at the grave of Capt William Leefe Robinson at Harrow Weald, 3 Sept 1989   *Photograph by the author*

17 Battle of Britain

On 9 June 1921, at East Ridgeway, Cuffley, hundreds of people attended the unveiling of a memorial in memory of Capt William Leefe Robinson, VC. The granite obelisk, erected with contributions raised by the *Sunday Express* newspaper, draped in a Union Jack, was attended by a military guard of honour. The young combat pilot had a special place in the hearts of many of the population who remembered with gratitude the ultimate sacrifice he had made for his countrymen and women.

Some years later the memorial was badly damaged by vandals who had torn the bronze wings from the plaque. It lay forgotten from the memories of a new generation excited by the promise of a new world of the twenties and thirties. War and its horrors faded from the everyday scene of daily life, only relived by the nightmares of those who had suffered life-long scars from the experience. The people of Great Britain were asleep to the menace of Adolf Hitler who, on 26 February 1935, created the new German airforce – the Luftwaffe, with one of Manfred von Richthofen's pilots, Herman Goring, as Commander-in-Chief. The Richthofen Squadron was re-born on 28 March 1935, equipped with He 51 biplanes. The squadron dropped its old title of SA, or 'Storm Troops', a title to be adopted later by a menacing and lethal military unit of the German Army. The squadron was to see battle in Spain under Lt-Col Wolfram von Richthofen. The Condor Legion, with fifty Junkers JU52s and fifty He51 escort fighters gave close support to General Franco's armies and was later to bomb England.

Meanwhile, over the peaceful fields of the English countryside, Hawker Furies, the open cockpit, biplane fighter, glinted like silver fish in the searchlights of mock battles, not twenty years after the hostilities of the 'War to end all Wars!' Fighter Command was formed on 6 July 1936, and the Priory at Bentley, near Stanmore, Middlesex, was set up as a Fighter Command Headquarters to serve throughout the Battle of Britain. The Hawker Hurricane fighter planes at that time suffered from the same fault that had been the downfall of Billy Robinson – the aircraft could not fly at altitudes above 15,000ft without the machine guns freezing up! In the spring of 1939, Supermarine Spitfires of No 65 and No 75 Squadrons formed part of a fighter unit at Hornchurch. Fitted with eight

Leefe Robinson Memorial, Cuffley   *Photograph by Ron Willis*

.303 Browning machine guns, a Rolls-Royce Merlin engine of over 1,000hp and with a maximum speed of 355mph at 19,000ft, there was no comparison with his machine's performance of 72mph at 6,500ft, with only a 90hp engine and one machine gun. The Spitfire was a formidable evolution from Robinson's BE2C.

Following the invasion of Poland by German armies on 1 September 1939, the Royal Air Force light bomber squadrons of the Advanced Air Striking Force and four Hurricane fighter squadrons allotted to the Air Component of the British Expeditionary Force crossed to France to do battle once again with the German airforce. By 16 May 1940 the armies of the British Expeditionary Force were ordered to evacuate France from the beaches of Dunkirk, and by 18 June the last British fighting planes left France. During that battle 320 British pilots were killed, reported missing or had died of injuries. 115 were taken prisoner of war and interned. Great Britain was left with 1,094 qualified pilots to face the might of the victorious German High Command.

For reasons that have remained a mystery, the Germans did not follow the victories in France with the immediate invasion of the British mainland and this gave Air Chief Marshal, Sir Hugh Dowding, Air Officer Commanding-in-Chief at Bentley Priory, time to recover sufficiently from his dilemma to plan the defence of Great Britain. The foundation laid by

Sir Hugh Dowding, Lord Swinton, the Secretary of State for War (1935-38), and the Air Ministry's foresight pre-war were tested to their full capacity in the lull before Fighter Command launched into the Battle of Britain in 1940. Air Chief Marshal, Sir Trafford Leigh-Mallory, Commander of No 12 Group, a leading tactician and Air Marshal Sir Keith Park, the brilliant defensive Commander of No 11 Group, were to play a leading part in the preparations. No 54 Squadron (Rochford) had joined the unit at Hornchurch.

On 10 July 1940 Fighter Command was fighting for its existence in the defence of Great Britain. At the end of that day 13 German aircraft were destroyed for the loss of 6 British aircraft. The battle for the skies over Britain lasted until 31 October 1940, and has been too well documented to be repeated by the author, but his own recollection as a schoolboy of 14 years is recalled from brief entries in a Beal Modern School (Ilford, Essex) exercise book shown at Appendix 5. Three years later, at Christmas 1943, the author was given a book by his girlfriend, now his wife, entitled *Sky Riders* – a book of Famous Flyers by Harry Harper, published by Collins, in which a photograph of Capt W Leefe Robinson, VC, brought back fond memories to his mother, Rose Bills, née Jones.

The memorial and Leefe Robinson's grave had fallen into disrepair and the memory of Billy faded with the passing years until 1986, when the *Daily Express* newspaper resurrected his fame, following complaints from readers, and made arrangements on the 70th anniversary of his victory to restore the memorial obelisk, commemorating for the second time 'the valour of a young pioneer airman who, in darkened skies above the site, brought down the first enemy airship destroyed over British soil'. A commemorative brochure was sponsored and produced by Welwyn Hatfield District Council in conjunction with the many well-wishers for the project. The unveiling was carried out on 2 September 1986, by Air Vice-Marshal M J D Stear, CBE, MA, RAF, Air Officer Commanding 11 Group and was attended by the Chairman of the Council, Bill Couzens. *Solemn Melody* by Walford Davies was played by the Central Band of the Royal Air Force under the direction of Squadron Leader H B Bingley, MBE, B.Mus (Lond.), LRAM, AROM, RAF. The ceremony was attended by many local dignatories, friends and relatives of the airman. The *Last Post* was sounded, following a few moments' silence, then *The Reveille*, and *The Royal Air Force March Past*.

103

Last photograph of Robinson at home, Dec 1918   *Christie's*

18 A Medal for Valour

In 1955 Regina Libin, daughter of Katherine Baroness Heyking and niece of Capt Leefe Robinson, inherited from her mother the 'Pip Squeak and Wilfred' medals awarded to her uncle, together with the Victoria Cross and various memorabilia. 'Gia' Libin, pleased with her new inheritance, agreed to the display of the treasurers at St Bees School, Cumbria, in memory of the days he spent as a pupil before joining the Army and, until 1970, they attracted the interest of both students and parents.

It is recorded at this time, and unknown to Mrs Libin, that a man persuaded a member of the school that he had authority to borrow the medals to assist in the writing of a book on the life story of Billy Robinson, and the medals promptly vanished. Gia was shattered by the news of the loss of the medals, and astonished at a caller, who admitted he was the 'culprit' and who audaciously asked to borrow Robinson's Victoria Cross to help him achieve a real atmosphere for the compilation of the draft manuscript, and in preparation for a film. Trustingly, and taken in by the charm of the stranger, Gia agreed to loan the precious 'medal for valour'. In succeeding months Gia's attempts to contact him were unsuccessful, until eventually she traced the person to a flat in Southgate, North London, just as the bailiffs arrived to repossess various goods! Realising her predicament, Gia swiftly left her motor car, entered the premises, searched, and successfully found the purple beribboned Cross.

Many years later, in 1980, she traced some of the memorabilia to the RAF Museum at Hendon, London. There she found Robinson's signalling pistol, fired after shooting down the Schutte-Lanz SL11, his escaper's hair-brush with the home-made compass concealed in the removable wooden back. The bent 1806 halfpenny which had saved him from a nasty wound over Lille in 1915 was proudly displayed in the showcase. The curator advised Mrs Libin that the museum had acquired them in 1976, but would not reveal the source.

At that time, Mr Roy Bartlett, a collector from Essex, bought Robinson's 1914-15 Star (2/Lt Worc.R.), British War Medal and the Victory Medal, MID Oakleaf (Capt) in good faith from a man for £1,500.

In July 1987, after 37 years teaching young children, Mrs Gia Libin retired from her vocation as Headmistress of a private school, and thought

seriously about raising money for a charitable Trust benefiting children suffering from leukaemia, and decided to enlist the help of Christie's of London to find the missing medals from the Collection. Enquiries made by Richard Bishop, Auctioneer and Association Director of the Coins and Medal Department of Christie's, came up with a Mr Bartlett who, eager to return the lost medals to the Victoria Cross, presented them to Mrs Libin stating, 'As a caring collector, I want them to be reunited with the VC.'

In November 1988, Christie, Manson and Woods Limited of King Street, St James's, London, publically announced to the media the sale of Orders, Decorations and Campaign Medals. 'To be sold at Christie's Great Sale Rooms on Tuesday, 22nd November, 1988, at 10.30am and 2.30pm precisely.'

The catalogue stated:

The Property of
MRS R.G. LIBIN

sold on behalf of

'A MEDAL FOR LIFE'
A charitable trust to benefit
children suffering from Leukaemia.

Lot 230

The Victoria Cross Group to Lieutenant later Captain William Leefe Robinson, Royal Flying Corps, late Worcester Regiment.

(a) Victoria Cross reverse of suspension bar inscribed 'Lieut. W L Robinson Worcestershire Regt.' RFC reverse centre of cross dated '2 & 3 Sept. 1916'.
(b) 1914-15 Star (2 Lieut Worc R).
(c) British War and Victory Medals MID oakleaf (Capt).
(d) Next-of-kin bronze plaque, the group good very fine.
(e) A comprehensive and most interesting collection of related memorabilia including the 'lucky half-penny' 1806, damaged Webley & Scott signal pistol, pieces from the German airship SL11 including a control wheel, temperature control switch, fabric section, part of a ply girder, two metal and three rubber pieces, a matchbox cover with portrait, travelling clock, wooden-back hair brush with concealed compass, RAF ensign, and a large quantity of letters, photographs, postcards, official documents, contemporary press cuttings, a newspaper billboard poster of the 5th September, 1916, announcing the award of the VC and other related literature.

Second Lieutenant Harold Leefe Robinson, 101st Grenadiers, Indian Army.

(a) 1914-15 Star (2 Lieut. IARO).
(b) British War and Victory Medals.
(c) Next-of-kin bronze plaque, the group good very fine.
(d) A small quantity of related photographs and documents.

London Gazette, 5 September 1916: 'For conspicuous bravery. He attacked an enemy airship under circumstances of great difficulty and danger, and sent it crashing to the ground as a flaming wreck. He had been in the air for more than two hours and had previously attacked another airship during his flight.

£60,000-80,000

An exhibition catalogue was available in colour and sepia tones, entitled 'The Life and Loves of Captain William Leefe Robinson VC, 1895-1918 – Royal Flying Corps'. The front cover displayed a painting of Billy Robinson in the uniform of the Royal Flying Corps, and advised of the sale for the Charitable Trust to benefit children suffering from Leukaemia and named 'A Medal for Life'.

The medals were also shown at the Leefe Robinson Restaurant at Harrow Weald, at which Squadron Leader H E Harvey, ex-patriot prisoner, aged 93 years, was present, who had been a fellow 'inmate' with Billy Robinson in 1917-18. Gia Libin, who recalled that both her parents died of cancer, advised newspaper men: 'As children have been very much a part of my life, I thought it appropriate to sell the medals and use the money to benefit children suffering from the same dreadful disease.'

The Auctioneer, Mr Bishop, sold lot 230 for a total of £98,000. The buyer was unknown to Christie's of London, and dealers at the sale were unable to help Gia to determine whether the medals would remain in Great Britain.

19 So Happy and Gay

The evening of Thursday, 15 October 1987, was dark, wet and cheerless, an extension of a day of torrential rain that had swept through the South and East of England. The wind tugged at the coat tails of the Chief Photographer of the *Sunday Express* newspaper as he bent to the gusts that whipped around the suburban conurbation of Basildon in the hamlet of Billericay, Essex. His mission, at the direction of Mr Dickinson, Deputy Editor, was to obtain from the author a photograph of Miss Rose Jones, a friend and companion of Billy Robinson during the First World War.

'Will you publish by the weekend?'

'Yes, hopefully this weekend's *Sunday Express.*'

'It was kind of the Editor to request a photograph of my mother, unfortunately the only photograph I have of Leefe Robinson is in a book.'

'Don't worry, he will obtain a good likeness from the archives, and they will appear together again after 70 years!'

'He laughed. 'Goodnight.'

'The wind is getting really fierce, what a lousy night! goodnight.'

Twenty miles distance to the south-east, the population of the township of Hadleigh was retiring to bed, thankful for the security of bricks and mortar to protect them from the gusting winds coming off the Thames Estuary; alert to the sounds of trees slapping against buildings and a noisy tin can being hurtled along the deserted street. The weathermen had warned of severe winds, but the town slept on into the night unaware of the approaching 'hurricane' sweeping along the South Coast of England. Gradually the wind force increased until the countryside was attacked by furious gale-force gusts that swept a path of destruction through towns and villages, uprooting trees, tearing tiles from roofs and toppling chimneys and garden walls like skittles in an alley. Power cables crashed down, causing lightning flashes that illuminated the inferno of noise and bedlam. The population cowered beneath the bed linen. Those who reluctantly got up to investigate, stumbled through the darkness of the failed National Grid electricity supply. Rose Bills, née Jones, 87 years old and a widow, terrified of falling slates from the roof of her small cottage, huddled beneath the bedsheets, unable to breath properly in her distress, gasping to gain air into her lungs. Her daughter, Joyce, hurriedly dressed and stumbled out into the street to call out the emergency doctor, but found the telephone in the kiosk dead – the trees around her thrashing wildly in the blackness of the raging storm. Finally, raising the doctor from a neighbour's telephone, she returned to the cottage to reassure her mother that help had been summoned. At the height of the storm Rose had suffered a mild heart-attack, a prelude to her death some three months later. The storm abated in the early hours of the morning light to reveal the most astonishing trail of destruction, the like of which had not been seen before in southern and eastern England.

On 18 October 1987, the following letter appeared in the 'Letters' column of the *Sunday Express*:

MOTHER'S DATE WITH A HANDSOME VC HERO
I read with interest your report of the sale of a VC awarded to Flight Sub-Lieut Warneford in 1951 for shooting down the first Zeppelin in the Great War and who died tragically a few days later in a flying accident. My mother, then Miss Rose Jones and sweet 17, sat wide eyed and beautiful at a restaurant table in Ilford in 1917 with a very handsome 21 year old aviator of the Royal Flying Corps. Lieut W Leefe Robinson who was stationed nearby.

In September 1916 he had shot down a Zeppelin at Cuffley, the first over British soil. He also was awarded the Victoria Cross and regrettably like his predecessor, was shot down by anti-aircraft fire* in 1917 and taken prisoner. He was put into solitary confinement where his health deteriorated and upon repatriation at the end of the war, he died of influenza.

My mother, now 87 years old, reminisces with a twinkle in her eye of the day the peas from her dinner plate shot across the floor of the restaurant in her nervousness at her tryst with a hero, recalling his masterful ordering of more peas to replace those she had lost.

* not proven.

(signed) Leslie W Bills
Billericay, Essex

The response to this letter was remarkable. The following Sunday the newspaper published a letter from a correspondent – Mr W F Corfield:

The delightful story of Rose Jones and Lieut W Leefe Robinson, VC last week reminded me of a sad prelude to the Zeppelin which he had shot down at Cuffley, Herts, behind The Plough public house.

Some 24 years ago I lived for a few years in the nearby village of Essendon in an old converted cottage. At the time, we shook our heads at our 13 year old daughter Anne when she told us that from time to time she awoke in the night to excited shouts and laughter of two girls in a field behind the cottage. We said she's been dreaming.

Talking to an old inhabitant one day he told me that two bombs had been dropped on the village from the doomed Zeppelin. One demolished an end wall of the church and the other had killed two young teenage sisters watching in a field behind my cottage and where they had lived.

I didn't tell my daughter until she had grown up.

(Signed) W F Corfield
Barnet, Herts.

The author received letters in reply from over 40 persons, who had been eye-witnesses to the destruction of the Zeppelin and who recalled vividly the excitement and agony of that moment. From Canada, New Zealand, and many parts of Great Britain, the interest in William Leefe Robinson had been kindled yet again, with bright clear images of seventy years ago.

From the Old Cottonian Association came the information that at Billy's school in Bangalore, South India, there had been a display of his flying uniform and a cap in the Boys' School dining hall, and these items were loaned to a local museum where 'they were attacked by white ants and they just disintegrated' . . . very sad indeed. A pilot in the Second World War who attended the school between 1924-32, told of Robinson's 'Sam Browne' belt in the showcase and that at each Armistice Day his name was always the first to be read in remembrance!

There was an intriguing letter from an airman who recalled – 'Towards the end of the first war I was in an RAF Squadron. Our CO at times 'phoned a lady and they talked of Lieut Leefe Robinson, whom they must have known was ill in prison. He also spent some time playing music on his drums to the lady. I only know because, in those days, the CO of a fighter squadron had little secrecy. If by some chance, your mother was the lady it may bring another twinkle!'

One apparently caring lady wrote from Watford of her visits to the Cemetery at Harrow Weald to the grave of her brother, who died in 1927, advising of the unkempt state of the graveyard and the nearby grave of William Leefe Robinson, VC. She remarked on the photograph in the newspaper, '. . . he looked so happy and gay, so please tell your mother, when I visit my brother's grave again, I will place some flowers on the Lieutenant's grave from her and me.'

Living in Durham, Ena wrote of the friendship of her brothers with Robinson and the family's hero worship for 'Young Billy' and his gallantry, recalling her sad loss of two of her six brothers at the Battle of the Somme Valley in the summer and autumn of 1916. The pleasant countryside had been entirely devastated by the battles that had raged over it, where the chalk soil of the district became a quagmire in wet weather and the fields reduced to a lunar landscape of mud-filled shell holes. Each soldier was expected to move up in fighting order into prepared trenches with steel helmet, rifle and bayonet, entrenching tool, two gas-helmets, wire-cutters, 220 rounds of ammunition, two sand bags, two Mills bombs, in addition to a regulation groundsheet, water bottle, haversack and field dressing. The weight carried by each man was in excess of 66lbs which not only made it difficult to get out of a trench, but almost impossible to advance much quicker than a slow pace, or to get down quickly, or to rise up again, having done so. In this situation the infantryman was required to advance against a heavily armed enemy.

'No braver or more determined men,' said a Brigadier-General, 'ever faced an enemy than those sons of the British Empire who went "over the top" on the 1st July 1916.' 60,000 British casualties was the price of the first day of the Somme battle.

The memories of 87-year-old Barbara, and her horror as an 18-year-old girl at the terrible death of the German airmen being burnt alive, and the 'Zeppelin' falling in flames. As an 18-year-old girl, the night of terror was still a vivid picture, and her recollection of the elation of the public at the sight of the destruction of the great airship sickened her.

Fond memories from Lily born in Ilford (Essex), but living in Leytonstone (London) at the time of the event, who over 70 years later still had a 'crush' on the handsome aviator, and who recalled the shrill siren and throb of 'Zeppelin' engines, and being hurriedly pushed under a table with her brother, as her mother and baby sister fled to the protection of the cupboard under the staircase. As the 'Zepp' caught fire, her concern for the German airmen was tempered by her confusion at her parents' elation over the 'brave British airman' who had saved the town from destruction. In later years, Lily's husband was killed in 1942 whilst serving in the RAF as a navigator.

Olive, who regularly took a short cut through the Harrow Weald cemetery, and was familiar with the gravestone of William Leefe Robinson, had often wondered what the airman had looked like. After seeing his photograph in the *Sunday Express*, she was now resolved in her desire to see that the stone memorial survived the ravages of time.

Lilian, from Cuffley, recalled her tantrum at not being awakened by her parents who had witnessed the spectacle of the airship inferno.

Harold, an ex-patriot Royal Marine, on holiday in England from New Zealand, had read the newspaper report in the *Sunday Express* and, sending his best wishes to 'Rosie', the author's mother, he wrote of his aunt, Alice Leefe, wondering if he was related to the family, as he was also a Robinson!

From Cheltenham, Marjorie, widow of an Imperial Airways pilot of circa 1936, quite rightly expressed the opinion that nothing had happened of any note in London since Pepys and the Fire of London in 1666, until that eventful night of 3 September 1916. Like the majority of ladies of her age, she was warmed by thoughts of Billy Robinson, and sent to the author a photograph of the airman, with the comment: 'I do hope your mother 'Rosie' (charming name) is well now and that she will like the enclosed photograph of her boyfriend of long ago – he is so extremely handsome. What a waste!'

20 Thora's Story

Thousands of miles away in British Columbia, another elderly lady called Thora penned memories of her childhood and of a very strange story circulating in Plaistow, near East Ham (London) in 1916, concerning the identity of one of the crew members of the ill-fated SL11 airship. His body was taken away from the other victims and buried overnight in a small park nearby, between Humerston Road and Masterman Road, East Ham. The military authorities declared the area 'out of bounds' to the public. Thora's parents were horrified to learn that the pretty little park at the bottom of their garden was suddenly closed to the public and a mysterious grave dug overnight. Who was the dead German and why was he buried away from the others? The authorities eventually released the name of the victim as Count von Zeppelin! The local population were infuriated; not only were they being bombed from the skies but their parkland was being taken from them and used as a burial place for the very man who had invented this killing machine. The 'battle' raged on between public and authorities, until one night the grave suddenly disappeared and the grass 'tidied up'. A newspaper reported that 'the body had been moved to another site and would be returned to Germany after the war'. The name of the dead person was not given.

In 1950 Thora emigrated to Canada, settling in Kimberley at the foot of mountains on the fringe of a huge forested area. She recalled being invited to write an article in 1982, on the anniversary of the Second World War 'D' Day, of her life and experiences at the War Office. She wrote of Lt Leefe Robinson's exploits and the love and respect felt by the British people at that time. She remembered and wrote of the mysterious crew member, and mentioned his name. The article caused a stir with the reading public of Kimberley, as it seemed that the name given to the British population in 1916 was incorrect and, after extensive research, the crew member then named was found to be still alive in 1979! Who then was buried in that grave, and was the body transferred to his fatherland years later? Information received from enquiries at the War Office neither confirmed nor otherwise that the mysterious German was a nobleman. Over 70 years later Thora was still haunted by this mystery. Who was the dead German? Why was he buried away from the others? The dead crew of the SL11 were all buried in a grave near Cuffley (Herts). [Author's note: One crew member of Zeppelin L31 was buried alongside Hauptmann Schramm and his crew.]

The author makes no apology for including further extracts from this remarkable lady's recollection of the past, and these are reproduced below:

It was my father who patterned my life for me through his own experiences of travelling, and being in the Boer War and the Afghanistan War, prior to my birth. He taught me to have great respect and love for all nationalities regardless of colour and race, and I can say that is almost a hobby with me today – I go out of my way to talk to them.

My earliest memories were when I was six years old in 1916, and I witnessed a Zeppelin coming down in flames. We moved to Bristol for the remainder of the 1914-18 war, where I used to go with an older cousin who was entertaining the wounded in hospital. The terrible sight of those men has remained with me ever since.

Returning to Essex in 1919 the next years were spent in a normal type education, and during those years I was able to be more involved with other nations. My father was an interpreter for the Indian Ambassador in London and that involved constant visitors to our house of Indian families – one daughter, Hinda, becoming a great friend.

During the years 1928-40 I had started out in business. One evening a week I returned to college to teach shorthand. I also became a licensed teacher of ballroom dancing at an academy, and also taught a class of young children dances of all countries.

At the age of 22 I was accepted by the Canadian Goverment (through the British Government) to be trained for nursing in the North West Territories – a job which was an ambition of mine. At the last moment the arrangements had to be cancelled – my father had a stroke and I was needed at home.

We then moved to the coast, Westcliff-on-Sea, Essex, just five minutes' walk from the beach. I have never been interested in any sports, but we had friends with a yacht and a speed boat. They seldom went out without me! I still enjoy the sport when I return to England.

In 1939 the horror broke over the world. Being under 40 I was conscripted for home duties, and I chose to be a conductress on a double-decker bus – I really enjoyed this unusual job. About this time the Military Authorities gave us 36 hours to leave our houses, together with all our belongings. This was necessary because Hitler was intending to invade England and the invasion would have started from the coast just about where we lived. Many houses were confiscated.

A few months later I was recommended for a secretarial position in CMHQ (Canadian Military Headquarters). As a senior secretary I was in the Top Secret Division and was chosen to do several top-secret jobs, one being the Minutes of all Allied Officers meetings. I was always the only female present, but was helped by interpreters. I also had to help a Russian scientist with his letters (on quick-drying runways for planes). We had to use our own idea of 'sign-language' since neither of us could speak the other's language.

After CMHQ making various enquiries about my personal life, I was assigned a special job, under strict armed guard. I had to type out on a printing machine a mass of information, although I was unaware of its meaning. Many months later I was called to a Top Secret meeting of Allied Officers where the Commander-in-Chief thanked me for my part in the 'D' Day plans. I then realised why I was not allowed to speak to strangers, nor discuss what I had been doing. Since I had the plan details in my head, I could have been a target for spies and the cause of the loss of thousands of men if I gave out any information.

One nasty experience I had. Civilians working at CMHQ had to carry trench helmets and army gas masks. We had a test in Trafalgar Square one day and out of hundreds of gas masks, mine was found faulty, causing a build-up of tear gas to be trapped in my mask. The army rushed me to hospital, but I was blind for three days.

Bombings were getting extremely heavy and continuous, so I volunteered for an air-raid warden's job for evenings and week-ends, and had to patrol the streets during raids. I lived 35 miles from the London office, and often the railway lines were bombed which necessiated detours on foot. I recall one instance when we had to pass through the town of West Ham early in the morning, which was still burning, and we (the passengers from the train) had to step over still burning bodies, separated limbs, etc. I had many close encounters with bombs and shrapnel because I had to be out of doors with the Wardens, but that was everyday life then.

As the war ended, I left CMHQ and became secretary to the Claims Manager at Lloyds of London – a job which was to help me later in Canada. Meanwhile, I got my degree in surgical chiropody and opened a surgery, as well as doing a year's nursing in Rochford (Essex) hospital.

Then death struck once again, so mother and I left for Canada (1950), where I became secretary to Lloyds Claims Assessor in Calgary, often assessing and settling marine claims myself.

In 1955 I personally became interested (not through any society) in the Stoney Indians in Morley, though I was actually concerned with the Band at Eden Valley, numbering 188. Over a six-year period, I spent many week-ends and holidays with them, putting on two big parties – June and December. They erected my own little teepee, and I took part in their tribal dances. As a 'blood-brother', they named me *Ya-hay-tu-sma*, meaning 'Mountain Dew' – dew causes crops to grow for their food, and *I* gave them food for *them* to grow.

In 1966 mother passed away (she was 91). I left Calgary and moved to Cochrane where I became secretary in the Fish and Wildlife Office for nearly nine years. Although I retired in 1975, I still keep in touch with the work as I love animals so much.

During 1968-86 I travelled a good deal; several times to Austria, Germany, Bavaria, Belgium; once to Holland and, of course, Britain often, and Malta and the Channel Isles later. Maybe a few of you reading this went through the horrors of bombing, a shortage of food, as well as I did, to say nothing of loss of family, so you know how I felt when landing in Calgary I was greeted by a friend who had just seen the 'Battle of Britain' film – she said: 'You really didn't go all through that did you? Wasn't it just propaganda to get more money to carry on the war?' Perhaps others thought that too!

In the late summer of 1988 the author met Thora when she was visiting from Canada, and dined with her and her cousin at the 'Golden Pheasant' Hotel in Burford, Gloucestershire. When she returned to Kimberley, she

115

wrote that she was looking after a friend's huge Siberian Husky dog, whom she 'found adorable', albeit that a neighbour had to take the animal out for walks as the powerful Arctic breed was too much for Thora's determined, but frail stature!

Charlie Fry and Daisy Jones, *c1918*   *Author's Collection*

21 Mike's Recollections

'Mike' Michell corresponded with the author following the *Sunday Express* article on Robinson's friendship with Rose Jones, on 18 October 1987. Later they met and Mike regaled the author with his recollections of the period when he was manager of the Jumboor Coffee Estate in the tiny Indian state of Co-org, and of the Robinson family. He also reminisced on his friendship with Billy Robinson's friend, Lt C S Irons, MC, one of the several pilots who took to the air on 3 September 1916 and tried to intercept the Schutte-Lanz during its attack on London. On that day Lt Irons, whose nickname was 'Kubbana' Irons, was enjoying a movie in the local picture house when a message was flashed onto the screen for all pilots to return to their stations. On reaching his airfield Irons found that he could not take up his own aircraft, so took off in another machine and headed for the combat zone. When he arrived the Zeppelin was already on fire and he was unable to get too near because of the intense heat. Returning to his airfield after the encounter, Irons crash-landed but, fortunately, escaped without serious injury – two other aircraft crashed with fatal results.

Had Billy Robinson survived, he may well have made his career as a coffee planter in the tiny state of Co-org, southern India, which he loved so dearly, as did 'Kubbana' Irons. Mike Michell believed that Iron's friend, Wing Commander (Huffey) Sprott, probably had some influence on Irons regarding his career after the First World War. Sprott's father had a coffee plantation in Co-org and the Wing Commander may have suggested that Irons go out to Co-org and learn to be a coffee planter.

Mike also recalled that the wife of Douglas Tweedie, the owner of Jumboor Coffee Estate, was in England at the time of the destruction of the SL11 Schutte-Lanz by Lt Robinson. She managed to obtain some souvenir pieces from the wreckage of the airship, which she took back to India, and these are still displayed in a cabinet in the Bamboo Club in Pollibetta, alongside Robinson's portrait.

Author's father, Sapper William Joseph Bills, E Corps Signals, 1916-18. Taken at Villers Bretonneux   *Author's Collection*

22 Past and Present

93 years old, Squadron Leader Hamilton E Hervey advised the author of his book *Cage Birds*, published many years ago by Penguin Books Limited, which tells the story of his imprisonment with Capt Wm Leefe Robinson during 1917-18, through four German prisoner-of-war camps. He never saw Robinson again after he was transferred from Clausthau to Holzminden.

In 1988, Peter Rose, Press Officer to Christie's, London, had hoped to arrange a meeting on television between the author's mother, Rose Jones, and Squadron Leader Hervey, both of whom had befriended Billy Robinson during his short life, as part of a publicity campaign in connection with the sale by auction of Robinson's VC and other memorabilia. Unhappily, Rose had died between the newspaper publication and Christie's publicity campaign.

*   *   *

Today, Regina Libin, the daughter of the eldest of Billy Robinson's sisters – Kitty – has perpetuated his memory in setting up the charitable trust 'A Medal for Life'. Kitty had married Baron Heyking in 1917, and they had two daughters, Rosemary, who did not survive, and Regina Gisela, who leads an active life in Sussex, and is now the Chairman of the trust fund for children suffering from Leukaemia.

Billy's sister Irene (who died in 1962) had married Lt Colonel T S Ross of the Indian Medical Service. They had two children, Harold Robert born 1917, and Mary Rose (now Mrs Rose David) born in 1923.

Sister Ruth, married to John Irwin, had two children. She lived to the age of 82 years.

Joan Whipple became the wife of Maj-Gen J M Brockbank in 1929. She died in December 1968.

Sir Frederick B Sowrey, KCB, CBE, AFC, has survived to this day and lives in Sussex.

Squadron Leader H E Hervey, who was brought down by anti-aircraft fire whilst flying a Nieuport Scout on 8 April 1917, now lives in Gt Billington, Beds, having reached the great age of 93 years. He still takes an active interest in the recording of the many historical facts of his confinement as a prisoner of war with Billy Robinson.

Ernest Robinson became a Major in the Indian Army and served until 1930. Afterwards he became curator of the RASC Museum at Aldershot until the late 1950s. He died in Surrey in 1963, aged 80 years.

Rose Jones married William Joseph Bills in 1919, and they lived in Romford, Chadwell Heath and Hadleigh, Essex. Rose had three children, the eldest son, the author; a daughter, Joyce, born 1930; and Leonard Edward, who died at 13 years. William Bills served in France and Belgium as a Sapper in the Royal Engineers and, after the First World War, became a senior lecturer at the Post Office Engineering School in London.

Of the Jones sisters and their young brother: Violet died 1978, Rose died in January 1988 (aged 87 years). The eldest sister, Daisy, still survives – a very bright 94-year-old – as has brother William – a young 84-year-old.

* * *

The passage of time has not dimmed the memories of many of the witnesses to the events of this story who still survive and who shared their memories with the author with remarkable clarity after more than 70 years. The author is indebted to all of them for their detail and assistance provided.

Epilogue

When all the world is young, lad,
And all the trees are green:
And every goose a swan, lad,
And every lass a queen.

Song from *The Water Babies* 'Young and Old' – Charles Kingsley.

It is nearly 75 years since Billy Robinson fought the foe over London, England, yet his image remains as bright today as it did at the time of his great victory over a dangerous and determined adversary. With selfless devotion for the protection of his country, we see in him the spirit and determination of many a young man, or woman to follow him in the cause of duty to country. He was the first of the few, to be followed by the Spitfire and Hurricane pilots of the Battle of Britain and many other gallant 'lads' and 'lasses' who gave their all in the protection of the British Isles.

Since Boadicea in ancient times we, as a nation, were not to be trifled with by any country who looked covetously at this Sceptred Isle. Napoleon said, 'the best thing between France and England is the sea,' but today we are building a channel tunnel to forge a tangible link between Europe and England.

However, the author recalls his father telling him the story of the retreat by the Allies in France in 1917. As a sapper in the Royal Engineers, exhausted and alone, he stumbled upon two retreating French soldiers, and together they shared their meagre rations. Later, in the shelter of a derelict barn, they sank into a fitful sleep. Early next morning his father awoke with a start to the sound of the guttural voices of advancing German infantrymen – not a hundred paces away. The Frenchmen had fled, leaving his father asleep to awake to his fate. Fortunately, he escaped, although he never forgave his 'allies'.

Nowadays, feats of brilliance are rare between countries, but the co-operation between England and France in creating an incredibly beautiful, bird-like, flying machine, which people, even now, gaze at in wonder, is encouragement for mankind. Concorde strikes no fear into the observer – is no instrument of war – neither a thunderous show of strength (as with the powerful engines of the RAF Red Arrows) – nor the menace of a Lancaster Bomber of yesteryear – but a great, friendly bird of perfection, a controlled determination by two countries to show the world their continued expertise in aircraft design, many years ahead of its time.

But, let us not forget our soldiers, sailors and airmen lost in past battles – we weep at the magnitude of the American cemeteries at Runnymede and Cambridge, the long lines of names, names and more names of Germans and Poles, each with their own secured piece of England.

Is the new European Community and the end of the 'Cold War' with the Eastern bloc nations the beginning of Peace for all mankind? Or just for Eastern and Western Europeans? That is what each fighting man and woman believed, each giving away a precious life to achieve stability for those left at home.

Twenty-five years after the author's mother befriended Billy Robinson, the German Luftwaffe dropped a landmine near to his family home in Chadwell Heath, Essex. As young children they were showered with bricks and glass but, fortunately, suffered no serious injuries. Fifty years later the author's granddaughter, Nichola, is learning German – hopefully our children will have the benefit of hindsight and the will to work towards 'Peace on Earth and Goodwill to ALL Men'.

'Age shall not weary them, nor the years condemn.
At the going down of the sun and in the morning
We will remember them.'

APPENDIX 1

Report on Night Patrol

From: Lieut. Robinson
Sutton's Farm
To: The Officer Commanding
39 H.D. Squadron

Sir,

I have the honour to make the following report on Night Patrol made by me on the night of the 2nd-3rd instant. I went up at about 11.8 p.m. on the night of the 2nd with instructions to patrol between Sutton's Farm and Joyce Green.

I climbed to 10,000 feet in 53 minutes. I counted what I thought were ten sets of flares – there were a few clouds below me but on the whole it was a beautifully clear night. I saw nothing till 1.10 a.m. when two searchlights picked up a Zeppelin about S.E. of Woolwich. The clouds had collected in this quarter and the searchlights had some difficulty in keeping on the aircraft. By this time I had managed to climb to 12,900 feet, and I made in the direction of the Zeppelin which was being fired on by a few anti-aircraft guns – hoping to cut it off on its way eastward. I very slowly gained on it for about ten minutes – I judged it to be about 800 feet below me and I sacrificed my speed in order to keep the height. It went behind some clouds avoided the searchlights and I lost sight of it. After 15 minutes fruitless search I returned to my patrol. I managed to pick up and distinguish my flares again. At about 1.50 a.m. I noticed a red glow in N.E. London. Taking it to be an outbreak of fire I went in that direction.

At 2.5 a.m. a Zeppelin was picked up by the searchlights over N.N.E. London (as far as I could judge).

Remembering my last failure I sacrificed height (I was still 12,900 feet) for speed and made nose down in the direction of the Zeppelin. I saw shells bursting and night tracer shells flying around it. When I drew closer I noticed that the anti-aircraft aim was too high or too low; also a good many some 800 feet behind – a few tracers went right over. I could hear the bursts when about 3,000 feet from the Zeppelin. I flew about 800 feet below it from bow to stern and distributed one drum along it (alternate New Brock and Pommeroy). It seemed to have no effect; I therefore moved to one side and gave it another drum distributed along its side – without apparent effect. I then got behind it (by this time I was very close – 500 feet or less below) and concentrated one drum on one part

123

(underneath rear) I was then at a height of 11,500 feet when attacking Zeppelin.

I hardly finished the drum before I saw the part fired at glow. In a few seconds the whole rear part was blazing. When the third drum was fired there were no searchlights on the Zeppelin and no anti-aircraft was firing.

I quickly got out of the way of the falling blazing Zeppelin and being very excited fired off a few red Very's lights and dropped a parachute flare.

Having very little oil and petrol left I returned to Sutton's Farm, landing at 2.45 a.m.

On landing I found I had shot away the machine gun wire guard, the rear part of the centre section and had pierced the rear main spar several times.

I have the honour to be
Your obedient servant
W.L. Robinson, Lieut.
No. 39 Sqdn. R.F.C.

124

APPENDIX 2

Of all the girls I've loved . . .

'There are so many [girls] that I like,
Yes, I love in a small way, that I really
can't tell you which is best, they are all best.'
Wm. Leefe Robinson

Some of Billy's girl friends and companions (alphabetically):

ALICE DELYSIA	(Actress at Folies Bergère & Moulin Rouge, 1916)
MRS FAIRFAX	(Nr York, early 1916)
VIOLET GRINLING	(Friend of Lt Sowrey)
MURIEL HOGG	(Journey to England, 1913)
DORIS IREDALE	(Schooldays, 1913)
RUBY JENKINSON	(Schooldays, 1913)
ROSE JONES	(Ilford, Essex, 1916)
KATHLEEN LENNOX	(Kenilworth, 1915)
MURIEL MUSKIN	(Sutton's Farm, 1916)
NANCIE NICHOLSON	(Later married Capt E.N. Clifton)
MADGE SAUNDERS	(Wife of Leslie Henson, 1916)
VERA STAMMERS	(Sutton's Farm, 1916)
HEATHER THATCHER	(Actress, 1916)
ETHEL WATERS	(Schooldays, 1913)
JOAN WHIPPLE	(Née Stapylton-Smith, Fiancée)
DOROTHY WISE	(Schooldays, 1913)
LADY DOCTOR	(Chesterfield, 1916)
TWO GIRLS	(Hotel Cecil, London)
AMERICAN GIRL	(Bournemouth, 1912)
'SWEET, PRETTY LITTLE GIRL	(Whitsand Bay Hotel, 1915)

'I think of other things other than "Kitty O'Flaherties".'*
'I often wonder what kind of girl I will at last pick up.'
Wm. Leefe Robinson

* Actress on London Stage

125

APPENDIX 3

Air Raids

The first aeroplane raid on England – 25 December 1914.

The principal night raids on London by aeroplane took place on the following dates:

1916	28 November – London (West End) – 9 injured
1917	7 May – North London – 3 killed
	13 June – 157 killed, 432 injured
	7 July – 59 killed, 193 injured
	September 4, 24, 25, 29 and 30
	October 1 and 31
	December 6 and 18
1918	28/29 January – 58 killed, 173 injured
	February 16 and 17
	7 March – known as the Starlight raid
	19 May – 32 German Aeroplanes, 7 brought down
	5 August – last Zeppelin raid on England

AIR RAIDS AND BOMBARDMENTS.
(16th December, 1914, to 17th June, 1918).

No. of Raids	Description.	Civilian Casualties.								Sailors and Soldiers.		Total Casualties.
		Killed.				Injured.						
		Men.	Women.	Children.	Total.	Men.	Women.	Children.	Total.	Killed.	Injured.	
51	Airship raids	217	171	110	498	587	431	218	1236	58	121	1913
57	Aeroplane raids	282	195	142	619	741	585	324	1650	238	400	2907
12	Bombardments from the sea	55	45	43	143	180	194	230	604	14	30	791
	Totals ..	554	411	295	1260	1508	1210	772	3490	310	551	5611

Observer, January 12th, 1919.

APPENDIX 4

Zeppelin Raids on Gt Britain 1915-18

1915

Jan. 19	Yarmouth & District (First Zeppelin Raid).
April 14	Blyth, Wallsend & South Shields.
April 15	Maldon, Essex and Lowestoft.
April 30	Raids on Ipswich and Bury St Edmunds.
May 10	Bombed Southend-on-Sea area (100 50lb bombs used).
May 16	Ramsgate raided.
May 27	Southend-on-Sea, 3 killed, 3 injured.
May 31	London's first Zeppelin raid and Essex and Kent – 7 killed including a child of eight returning from a 'picture palace' with a 16-year-old girl friend – 33 injured – great damage to houses.
June 4	Raids on Essex, Kent, East Riding Yorkshire – several persons injured.
June 6	Hull, Grimsby and East Riding – 24 killed and 38 injured.
June 7	One of the returning airships, the LZ 37 was shot down in flames over Ghent by 24-year-old Flight Sub-Lt Reginald Alexander Warneford, Royal Naval Air Service, for which he was awarded the Victoria Cross. In a Parasol-winged Morane Saliner aircraft he dropped hand bombs on the Zeppelin until it was set ablaze. The explosion threw his aircraft over and he made an emergency landing behind enemy lines, re-started the engine, took off and returned to his airfield. He received the *Croix de Guerre* and the *Legion d'honneure* from the French Minister of War. Two days later the heroic airman was killed.
June 9	Squadron of Airships raided Norwich in fog. One Zeppelin damaged by gunfire from the ground batteries which landed in the North Sea and was towed towards Ostend. He was attacked by French seaplanes from Dunkirk, who dropped bombs on the stricken craft destroying it completely. The French then attacked the port of Ostend dropping 49 bombs on the German naval vessels – 35 persons were killed in England.

August 12	Raids on East Coast of England by two Zeppelins – 30 persons killed/injured – 14 houses destroyed.
August 17	Eastern Counties raided by three airships. One badly damaged by a British motor gun – 10 civilians killed – 48 injured.
Sept. 8	Raid on London, factories and harbours attacked, estimated damage £500,000 – 20 killed – 86 injured.
Sept. 12	(The ace German Capt Mathy commanded one ship which returned to its base.)
Sept. 13	Further raids on London.
Oct. 13	London and Eastern Counties – 56 killed – 114 injured.

1916

Jan. 31	Nine Zeppelins attacked Midland Counties, Norfolk, Suffolk, Lincolnshire, Leicestershire, Derbyshire, Staffordshire – 70 killed – 113 injured – L.19 forced into sea.
March 5	Three Zeppelins (L.11, L.13 and L.14) bombed York, Lincoln, Rutland, Huntingdon, Cambridge, Norfolk, Essex and Kent – 18 killed – 52 injured (one dockshed and a crane blown up at Hull).
March 31	Five Zeppelins raided Lincolnshire, Essex and Suffolk. Zeppelin L.15 sunk in Thames Estuary, after damage by Essex aircraft and gunfire. Crew surrendered to HMS *Olivine* – 48 killed and 64 injured including 31 soldiers of 3rd Manchesters billeted in a chapel at Cleethorpes, from a bomb dropped by L.22.
April 1	Raid on Sunderland by L.11 and L.17 – 22 killed – 130 injured.
April 2	Raid on Edinburgh by L.14 and L.22. Raid on Ipswich – 13 killed – 24 injured.
April 5	Raid on two ships off Bishop Auckland, Hull, Skinningrove – Laboratory and ironworks destroyed – 1 child killed (in Durham) – 9 injured.
April 24	Ten Zeppelins took off, eight reached England – 1 killed – 1 died of shock.
April 25	Five Zeppelins raid on East Suffolk, Essex, Kent and London (Leefe Robinson intercepted one).
April 26	One Zeppelin over Kent – no casualties.
May 2	Nine Zeppelins raid on Scotland, Yorkshire and Northumberland – 9 killed – 30 injured. L.20 caught in storm on return flight and crashed into a hill near Sandnaes, Stavanger, Norway. Broke in two.

July 28	Nine super-Zeppelins approached England together with The Old L.13 which alone crossed the coast South of the Humber at Boston – no casualties.
August 8	Raid by nine airships between the Wash and Tweed. L.24 dropped bombs on Hull killing 10 and injuring 11. L.11 bombed Whitley Bay injuring 3 children and 2 adults.
August 23	One Zeppelin dropped 34 bombs but little damage – no casualties.
August 24	Four raiders on East Suffolk, Essex, Kent. L.13 reached London bombed Millwall, Blackheath, Deptford, Eltham, Greenwich and Plumstead – 9 killed – 40 injured, extensive damage to residential property. L.32 intercepted by aircraft.
Sept. 2/3	Sixteen Naval and Military airships – 14 crossed the English coast. Object to attack London and Midlands. 4 killed – 12 injured. L.22 dropped bombs in fields – L.13 destroyed 3 gasometers at East Retford. Schutte Lanz SL.11 destroyed at Cuffley by Lt W. Leefe Robinson.
Sept. 23/24	Raid by 11 airships on London (3 Super Ships L.31, L.32 and L.33) Zeppelin L.32 brought down in flames by Lt Frederick Sowrey, and L.33 intact by Lt A de Bath Brandon. 11 killed – 25 injured. L.31 returned home commanded by Capt Mathy. 22 killed – 75 injured.
Sept 25	Seven Zeppelins raided England, included Dover – Four over Yorkshire, Lancashire and Lincolnshire. Bolton bombed. 13 killed – 10 wounded. L.22 bombed Sheffield. 29 killed – 21 wounded. L.14 bombed York. Little damage.
October 1	Zeppelin L.31 brought down in flames at Potters Bar by Lt Wm. J. Tempest – 11 airships – 10 reached England. L.14, L.16 raided Lincolnshire – L.24 London, but only reached Hitchin, killing one man. L.34 The Midlands. L.17 Norwich.

| Nov. 27/28 | Nine Zeppelins (Naval) raided England – L.24 to Tyneside with L.34, L.35, L.36 Super Zepps – L.34 intercepted by Lt Peyot. Dropped 16 bombs. Damaged 40 houses – killing 4 – injuring 34. Shot down in flames into sea West Hartlepool. |

L.16 bombed Wakefield and Chesterton (stayed over England for nine hours, despite two attacks by British aeroplanes).

L.21 bombed the Midlands but on return journey fighter planes attacked her and she was damaged by anti-aircraft fire. Over the Norfolk coastline she appeared to stop to repair her damaged structure. Outward bound across the North Sea at 8,000ft she was attacked by four aircraft and an armed trawler. The Zeppelin was finally destroyed by fire from the machines flown by Lt E. Cadbury and Sub-Lt G.W.R. Fane and E.L. Pulling.

1917

| June 16 | Zeppelin brought down off Kent Coast. |

| October 19 | Raid East and North East Coast and London – four airships destroyed. Many killed and injured in Piccaddilly Circus. |

1918

| April 12/13 | Last airship raid over England. |

APPENDIX 5

Air Raids

Observations taken by the author – aged 14 years.
'Somewhere in England' (actually Chadwell Heath near Hornchurch, Essex)

August 1940

Thursday 15th	7.15pm until 7.35pm.
Friday 16th	12.15pm until 1.10pm and 5pm until 6.10pm.
Sunday 18th	1.00pm until 2.00pm.
Friday 23rd	3.30am until 4.00am and 9.30pm until 10.15pm. Raider in searchlight. It was fired on. No sirens.
Saturday 24th	8.15am until 9.15am and 3.30pm until 4.20pm. On coming out of pictures, formation of enemy bombers came over the top of us. I clearly saw them. They were driven off by gunfire.
Sunday 25th	10.30pm until 11.30pm and 12.30am until 1.00am.
Monday 26th	3.30pm until 4.05pm. Saw three enemy bombers high in clouds being chased by Spitfires. 9.30pm until 3.30am.
Tuesday 27th	9.30pm until 12.10am. 3 bombs dropped. One in Jubilee Avenue, Romford.
Wednesday 28th	12.30am until 1.20am and 9.00pm until 4.15am. Saw flares dropped.
Friday 30th	11.50am until 12.33am, 3.00pm until 4.15pm, 4.50pm until 5.50pm and 8.45pm until 4.00am.
Saturday 31st	8.30am until 9.10am, 11.15am until 11.30am and 1.10pm until 2.00pm. Saw dog fight and shell bursts through my telescope. Also 6.00pm until 7.20pm. Two German planes came down at the same time. The Messerschmitt 109 came down behind Whalebone Guns. The pilot came down near Whalebone Bridge, Chadwell Heath, by parachute (2). The other plane is believed to be a Messerschmitt 109. Both pilots baled out. A Spitfire pilot that baled out at the same time was shot at and wounded by the LDV*. Also saw dog fights and gunfire. Also 10.00pm until 4.00am.

*Local Defence Volunteers, later Home Guard.

September 1940

Sunday 1st	11.10am until 12.20pm and 2.00pm until 3.15pm.
Monday 2nd	8.10am until 9.10am and 4.15pm until 6.00pm. Saw 100 German aircraft go through a barrage of gunfire. Also 11.20am until 3.00am.
Tuesday 3rd	10.22am until 11.30am and 3.00pm until 4.00pm and 11.40pm until midnight.
Wednesday 4th	9.15am until 9.50am, 1.30pm until 1.50pm and 9.15pm until 10.50pm (3 parachutes dropped out of a bomber. 10 flares (red and white) Germans in searchlights).
Thursday 5th	10.00am until 11.00am, 2.50pm until 4.20pm and 9.20pm until 5.30am.
Friday 6th	8.45am until 10.00am, 6.00pm until 6.40pm, 9.00pm until 11.20pm and 11.50pm until 4.00am.
Saturday 7th	5.10pm until 6.40pm and 8.30pm until 4.50am.
Sunday 8th	12.30pm until 12.45pm and 8.00pm until 5.15am.
Monday 9th	5.15pm until 6.15pm and 8.45pm until 6.00am.
Tuesday 10th	1.00pm until 1.20pm, 4.00pm until 4.20pm, 5.15pm until 5.45pm, 6.00pm until 6.15pm and 8.15pm until 4.45am.
Wednesday 11th	1.00pm until 1.15pm, 3.30pm until 4.50pm, 5.10pm until 6.20pm and 8.45pm until 5.40am. (Shell fire all night)
Thursday 12th	4.45pm until 5.45pm and 9.15pm until 6.00am.
Friday 13th	7.45am until 8.45am, 9.50am until 2.00pm, 4.00pm until 4.15pm and 9.00pm until 5.30am.
Saturday 14th	9.15am until 10.00am, 11.05am until 11.20am, 3.55pm until 4.50pm, also a raid all night.
	N.B. owing to about 6 air raids each day, I will only write down things of interest.
Sunday 15th	During the night air raid, the Home Guard told us we had to get out because there was a time bomb in Mrs Judd's garden. We had to go in a public shelter all night. (We found out afterwards that a 250lb bomb had gone through Mrs Judd's box-room roof, came out of the side of the house, made a crater on the pavement and shot across the road and hit a house in our road. The bomb did not explode.
Tuesday 17th	Piece of shrapnel went through our greenhouse.

Wednesday 18th	During the night there were six high explosives dropped. One 70ft away from our front garden which burst the gas and water mains. One bomb demolished Stan's house next door. Further up Birchdale Gardens, Chadwell Heath, another house had a bomb to itself.
Sunday 22nd	A Junkers 88 of the Yellow Nose Squadron flew over at about 2,000ft. It was shot down by 2 Spitfires.

October 1940

Saturday 5th	An incendiary bomb was dropped near the signal box.
Tuesday 15th	Three tiles off roof.
Thursday 17th	A landmine dropped in the Bakers during the late evening. Another was dropped at the same time near Whalebone Lane along the High Road, this demolished a great many shops and a school. Some casualties. one man killed. We were more fortunate: our landmine was caught up in a tree (it was found by Mr Wiffen). Dad and I were standing at the back door and remarked, when the other landmine exploded, that they had brought up a new gun! After the landmine in the Bakers had been found, everybody was cleared out except one block of houses of which we were one. We slept peacefully all night, unaware of the landmine and after the mistake had been found out we were hurriedly cleared out. The mine was disabled by the Naval Authorities.
Saturday 26th	1 bomb dropped on Cedar Park Gardens, Chadwell Heath.

February 1941

Sunday 9th	2 bombs dropped in High Road.

April 1941

Sunday 20th Hitler's birthday	Just after coming off firewatching, a landmine dropped the other side of the station (Chadwell Heath) and this time went off. It damaged our house – back door off, living room frame out, windows blown out, slates off roof, ceiling down in Mum's room, rafter moved out of place in roof, and bathroom peppered with glass. I was asleep in front room and did not wake up! Mum (Rose Jones) screamed at me, thinking I had been hurt – the bed was covered in glass fragments.
	Spent Sunday putting tiles on roof.

133

APPENDIX 6

German Rank Comparisons with the British Military

Oberstelermann	Colonel
Maj (Major)	Major
Rittm (Rittmeister)	Cavalry Captain
Hpt (Hauptmann)	Captain
Oblt (Oberleutnant)	Lieutenant
Lt (Leutnant)	2nd Lieutenant
Fw Lt (Feldwebel Leutnant)	Warrant Officer
Vfw (Vizefeldwebel)	Sergeant-Major
Fl (Fleiger)	Enlisted Pilot
Uffz (Unteroffizier)	Corporal
Gefreiter	Lance Corporal
Obermaschinist	Upper Mechanic
Untermaschinist	Lower Mechanic

*The following pages have been taken
from Leefe Robinson's pocket diary.
Their bloodstained, battered and
sometimes illegible condition reflects
the ravages of the 1914-18 campaign*

CONVENTIONAL SIGNS & LETTERING
USED IN MILITARY FIELD SKETCHING.

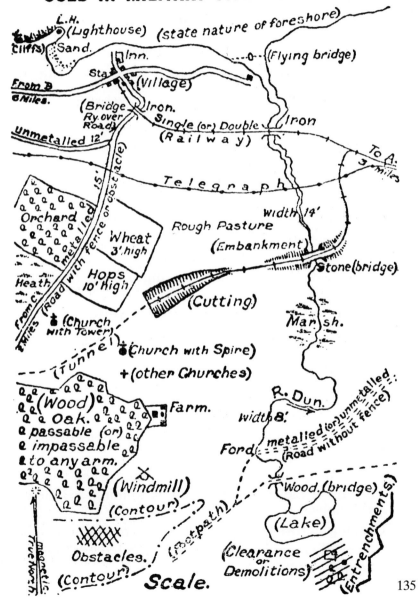

135

APPENDIX 8

Hints for Judging Distances.

Judging distances is a branch of a soldier's work which can be readily acquired, but which requires practice.

Never make a wild guess at a distance, have some such method as is given in the following :—

At 50 yards a person's mouth and eyes can be clearly seen.

At 100 yards a person's eyes appear like dots.

At 200 yards all parts of the body, badges, etc., can be seen.

At 300 yards the face is indistinct.

At 400 yards the movements of the legs can be made out.

At 500 yards the head and hat can be seen and colours distinguished.

At 600 yards the head is like a dot.

At 700 yards it is difficult to distinguish the head.

Points to be observed.

The distance is usually over-estimated when—

Looking over broken ground.

In a dull light.

Object is in the shade.

Heat haze is rising from the ground.

Both background and object are the same colour.

Kneeling or lying down.

The distance is usually under-estimated when :—

The air is clear and the sun is shining brightly on the object.

Looking across level ground, snow, or water,

Colour of object is different from the background.

Looking uphill or down.

136

Penetration of Rifle Bullet.

Material	Maximum Penetration.	Remarks.
Steel plate, best hard	$\frac{7}{8}$ inch ...	At 30 yards normal to plate.
Steel plate, ordinary mild or wrought iron	$\frac{3}{4}$ inch ...	$\frac{3}{8}$ inch is proof at not less than 600 yards, unless the plate is set at a slope of $\frac{3}{4}$, when $\frac{3}{8}$ inch is proof at 250 yards.
Shingle	6 inches ...	Not larger than 1 inch ring gauge.
Coal, hard ...	9 inches.	
Brickwork, cement mortar	9 inches ...	150 rounds concentrated on one spot will breach a 9-inch brick wall at 200 yds.
Chalk	15 inches.	
Brickwork, lime mortar	14 inches ...	9-inch brick wall at 200 yards.
Sand, confined between boards, or in sandbags	18 inches ...	Very high velocity bullets have less penetration in sand at short than at medium ranges.
Earth, free from stones (unrammed)	40 inches ...	Ramming earth reduces its resisting power.
Soft wood—*e.g.*, fir with grain	58 inches ...	Penetration of brickwork and timber is less at short than at medium ranges.
Hard wood—*e.g.*, oak with grain	38 inches.	
Clay	60 inches ...	Varies greatly. This is the maximum for greasy clay.
Dry turf and peat	80 inches.	

Rifle Definitions.

Axis of the Barrel (AB) is an imaginary line following the centre of the bore from the breech to muzzle.

Line of Sight (CDE) is a straight line passing through the sight and the point you aim at.

Line of Fire (BE) is a line joining the muzzle of the rifle and the target.

Line of Departure (BF) is the direction of the bullet on leaving the muzzle.

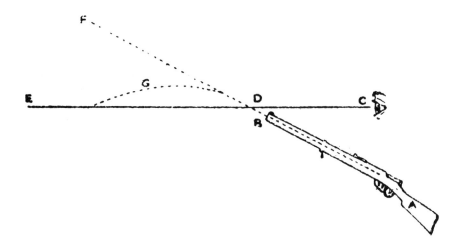

The Trajectory (DGE).—The curved line travelled by the bullet in its flight.

The Culminating Point (G) is the greatest height above the line of sight to which the bullet rises in its flight ; this is reached at a point a little beyond half the distance to which the bullet travels.

The First Catch is that point where the bullet has descended sufficiently to strike the head of a man, whether mounted, kneeling, standing, lying, etc.

Rifle Definitions—*continued.*

The First Graze is the point where the bullet, if not interfered with, will first strike the ground.

The Dangerous Space is the distance between the first catch and the final graze.

Gravity.—The natural attraction which draws all unsupported bodies towards the earth.

Calibre.—The diameter of the bore of the rifle in inches measured across the lands.

Collective Fire.—The fire of several rifles combined for a definite purpose under the orders of a fire leader.

Beaten Zone.—The belt of ground beaten by a zone of fire.

Foreground.—That portion of a field of fire lying nearest the origin of fire.

Field of Fire.—Any area of ground exposed to the fire of a given body of troops or group of guns.

Drift.—The constant deflection of the bullet due to the rotation imparted by the rifling. With Rifle, Short M.L.E., the drift is to the left.

Dead Ground.—Ground which cannot be covered by fire.

Oblique Fire.—When the line of fire is inclined to the front of the target.

Cover.—Concealment from view or protection from fire, or a combination of both.

Grazing Fire.—Fire which is parallel, or nearly so to the surface of the ground.

Individual Fire.—Fire opened without orders from a fire leader.

Enfilade Fire.—Fire which sweeps a target from a flank.

Rifle Definitions—*continued*.

Frontal Fire.—Fire the line of which is perpendicular to the front of the target.

Horizon.—The circle bounding the view where earth and sky appear to meet.

Traverse.—A bank of earth erected to give lateral cover.

Trench.—The excavation in a field work from which men fire.

Muzzle velocity.—The velocity in feet per second with which the bullet leaves the muzzle.

Abatis.—An obstacle formed of trees or branches picketed to the ground with their points towards the enemy.

Embrasure.—An opening in the parapet of a work through which a gun is fired.

Fascine.—A long bundle of brushwood tied up tightly, used for revetting, etc.

Gabion.—An open cylinder of brushwood, sheet-iron, etc., used in revetting.

Glacis.—The ground round a work outside the ditch

Head Cover.—Cover against frontal or oblique fire for the heads of men when firing.

Jump.—The movement and vibration of the rifle barrel, caused by the explosion of the charge and the passage of the bullet along the spiral grooves of the barrel.

Ricochet.—Bullets which rebound after striking the ground or other obstacle and continue their flight.

Rifling.—The spiral grooves cut down the inside of the bore of the rifle.

APPENDIX 10

Aeronautical Terms and their Meaning.

DEFINITIONS.

Aeroplane ... ... A flying machine heavier than **air.**

Aviator ... ... The pilot or driver of an aeroplane.

Biplane ... ... An aeroplane with two sets **of** main planes one above the other.

Monoplane... ... ... An aeroplane with one set of main planes.

Nacelle ... ... The car of a balloon or dirigible. An enclosed shelter for the pilot of a biplane.

Staggered planes... A biplane or triplane in which the upper planes are set in advance of the lower.

Tractor machine ... An aeroplane having its propellor in front.

Pusher ... ... An aeroplane having propellor in rear.

Triplane ... ... An aeroplane with three sets of main planes one above the other.

COMMON EXPRESSIONS.

A machine " rising " is said to be " climbing."

A machine descending without the engine running is said to " gliding " or " volplaning."

A machine descending too steeply is said to be " diving " or " vol pique."

A machine descending too flat and so losing flying speed is said to be " doing a pancake."

A machine " banking " describes the angle taken up by the planes when turning.

BALLOON TERMS.

Rigid... ... ... A term applied to a dirigible balloon whose envelope is provided with a stiff framework to keep it in shape.

Semi-rigid ... A term applied to a dirigible balloon which maintains its shape partly by the assistance of a suitable framework.

141

Station Signals.

To move **Signaller**	R L H O	Move to the right. Move to the left. Move higher or further off. Move lower or closer in.
Separate flags	8 F	When the flags of two signallers are crossing each other.
Use blue or white flag	B F W F	Semaphore or Morse flags.
Who are you?	R U	To find if signalling party is friendly or hostile.
Are you ready?	K Q	Sent if you have reason to think that the signaller is *not* ready.
Wait **No answer expected**	M Q DD, DD	Used for a temporary delay. If unable to receive owing to moving off, etc.
Send DD, DD messages	N A	See above.
No more messages at present	N N	Keep a good look out till you receive this signal.
Come in	C I	Used for instructional purposes " Come in and check."
Open light, or hold up flag	O L	
Turn off extra light	T O L	Used when desired to re-set lamp or helio.
Send slower	8 8	

Except where stated, all the above are used in both
Morse and Semaphore systems.

Badges of Rank.

Distinguishing Badges of Rank and Appointments worn in the British Army.

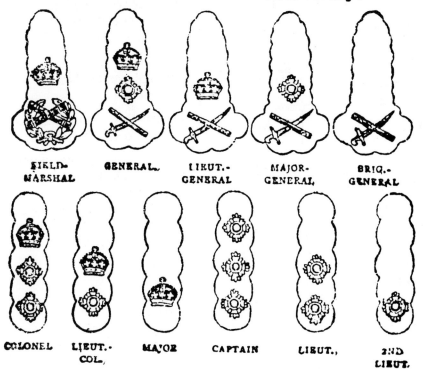

FIELD-MARSHAL	GENERAL	LIEUT.-GENERAL	MAJOR-GENERAL	BRIG.-GENERAL

COLONEL	LIEUT.-COL.	MAJOR	CAPTAIN	LIEUT.,	2ND LIEUT.

As all Soldiers are expected to salute any of His Majesty's Officers, it is necessary that they should be able to recognise one at once. The above clearly show you the shoulder badges worn by officers when in coloured uniforms (or dark great coats). When in Khaki, the above badges are worn on the cuff of both sleeves (on the shoulder when wearing great coat).

You can also recognise some of the officers of higher rank by their caps. The embroidery of the peaks of forage-caps is "oak-leaf" all round for Field-Marshals and General Officers ; oak-leaf on front edge for Field Officers on Staff of Army ; plain gold for Field Officers on cadre of a unit or department ; and black oak-leaf for Field Officers of Rifle Regiments. All other Officers wear a plain peak.

APPENDIX 12

Unveiling of the "Daily Express" Memorial to the Late Captain William Leefe Robinson V.C., R.F.C.
June 9, 1921, at 3·30 p.m.

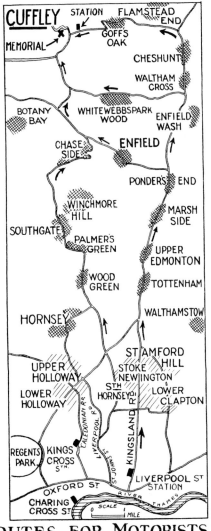

Routes for Motorists from London to Cuffley

St. Bees School Chapel.

THE UNVEILING OF
A TABLET

To Commemorate the Valour

of

WILLIAM LEEFE ROBINSON, V.C.

JOHN FOX-RUSSELL, V.C.

RICHARD WILLIAM LESLIE WAIN, V.C.

Saturday, June 18th, 1932,

AT 12 NOON.

APPENDIX 14

**From the Commemorative Brochure Sponsored and Produced
by Welwyn Hatfield District Council**

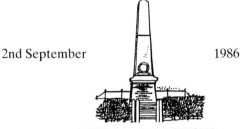

2nd September   1986

MUSICAL SELECTIONS
The Central Band of the Royal Air Force
Conducted by Sqdn Leader H B Hingley MBE, B.Mus(Lond), LRAM, ARCM, RAF

Solemn Melody . . . Walford Davies
The Civic and Ceremonial representatives take their places at the memorial

INTRODUCTION

**The Chairman of Welwyn Hatfield District Council
Councillor Bill Couzens**
will welcome those present and introduce the proceedings

THE UNVEILING

**Air Vice-Marshal M J D Stear CBE, MA, RAF
Air Officer Commanding 11 Group**
will unveil the restored memorial

MOMENT OF REMEMBRANCE

**The Revd. James C Sykes MA,
Vicar of St Andrew's, Cuffley**

Wreath Laying
There will follow wreath laying at the memorial, led by
the Chairman of the District Council

Followed by a short silence for remembrance, there will be sounded:

THE LAST POST

Then will be sounded:

THE REVEILLE

(Those present are asked to remain in their places until
the departure of the Civic and Ceremonial representatives)

The Royal Air Force March Past . . . Walford Davies/O'Donnell

APPENDIX 15

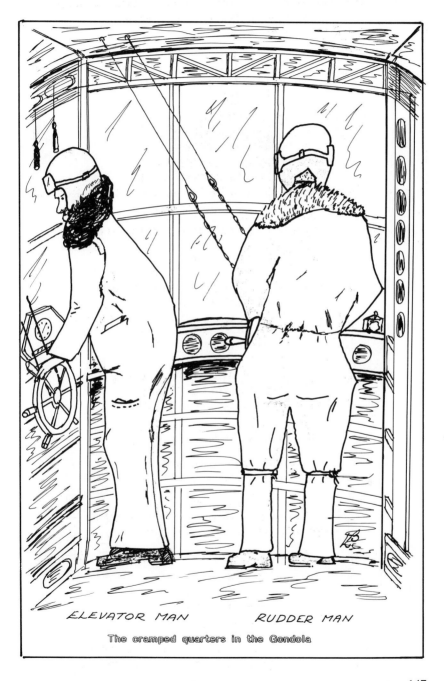

ELEVATOR MAN   RUDDER MAN

The cramped quarters in the Gondola

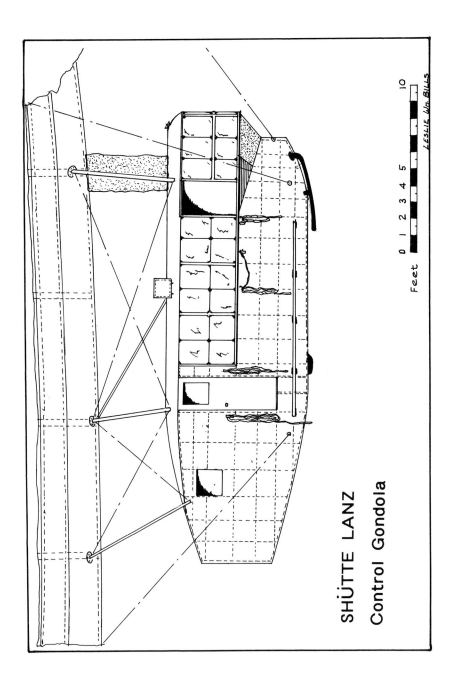

SHÜTTE LANZ

Control Gondola

Feet

0 1 2 3 4 5 10

LESLIE Wm BILLS